T0165002

NICK ARBOREA

The Spirit of

PAN

Passion Amore Nature

The most fascinating story you'll ever read about love, life, and the mystery of reincarnation.

BALBOA.
PRESS
A DIVISION OF HAY HOUSE

Balboa Press books may be ordered through booksellers or by contacting:

Balboa Press
A Division of Hay House
1663 Liberty Drive
Bloomington, IN 47403
www.balboapress.com.au
1-(877) 407-4847

ISBN: 978-1-4525-0418-6 (sc)
ISBN: 978-1-4525-0422-3 (e)

Because of the dynamic nature of the Internet, any web addresses or links contained in this book may have changed since publication and may no longer be valid. The views expressed in this work are solely those of the author and do not necessarily reflect the views of the publisher, and the publisher hereby disclaims any responsibility for them.

The author of this book does not dispense medical advice or prescribe the use of any technique as a form of treatment for physical, emotional, or medical problems without the advice of a physician, either directly or indirectly. The intent of the author is only to offer information of a general nature to help you in your quest for emotional and spiritual well-being. In the event you use any of the information in this book for yourself, which is your constitutional right, the author and the publisher assume no responsibility for your actions.

Any people depicted in stock imagery provided by Thinkstock are models, and such images are being used for illustrative purposes only.
Certain stock imagery © Thinkstock.

Printed in the United States of America

Balboa Press rev. date: 03/21/2012

CONTENTS

This book is dedicated to my late, dearest mum, Camilla Arborea, who gave me life and creativity. She passed away on April 28, 2011, not living to see it published.

To the greatest love of my life, my friend Annick, a woman whose company
I will always miss so dearly, and also to her daughter Grace.

To my nephews and nieces for when they are old enough to read about Uncle Nick's love life and family history.

And to all those who thought I was a dreamer.

Please find in this book the revelation of a mystery which has followed my life for centuries, believe it or not.

To discover it, you must read it. Enjoy.

Nicholas Arborea

To all these women who have left me something to remember them by, and to all those others I could not mention, thank you for sharing a moment of your life with me. In my heart and mind, you'll be with me until the end of time.

Nicholas Arborea

INTRODUCTION

Why did I write this book? I was encouraged by women to do it, years ago after they'd read my first novel, *Why Roses Have Thorns*. They thought I would have an interesting story to tell, which would be more appealing to read than an autobiography written by a self-absorbed footy idiot, a reformed presumed criminal, or any other celebrity fallen in disgrace.

But then one could say that there wouldn't be too many books written out there if the author didn't like to brag a bit about himself, his private life, and a subject that too many people wouldn't be comfortable to discuss with the general public.

I strongly believe that you don't have to be a rich and famous actor or a rock star to be entitled to tell your story. They had all the good luck in life to find the contacts that helped them get there and then they blew it all out of their sheer madness before being given a second chance in life. The self-inflicted problems and dysfunctional lives of stars are not more or less important to read than ours. Each of us has a story to tell, and you'd have to be a hypocrite to disagree.

If I was to worry beforehand that my story may stir some controversy with feminists and women who feel that they are the only victims in love, I wouldn't be writing this book.

After reading about one of the latest "sexiest men alive" boasting about himself, I finally decided to put pen on paper and here it is—the romance of Nick, a man some called *l'artista*. Now they all know the mystery behind my life—why I didn't get married and why

I couldn't end up with any of them. We may never understand why some things in life happen to us, until we discover why they do.

There you are, Laura. I finally wrote it for you!

Hi Nick,

Why don't you write something about your life on your experiences as a migrant?

Laura

PROLOGUE

Do you believe that you have a soul that never dies, that you may return and reincarnate?

In the early '30s, a world of women worshipped him at a time when women were allowed to only love one man. Sexual freedom was taboo.

This rule, though, only applied to desperate housewives.

Sex and the city was for the aristocratic circles, the divas married to the well-to-dos, to men who didn't have time for them, those who went to parties where they still today hide behind the mask.

He was the first "sexiest man alive" of the silver screen of Hollywood movies. The cinema then was black and white, just like the people of that time, genuine as they should be.

The dialogue was romantic, sensual, and stirred one's imagination.

You could only fantasise by the scenes that showed what he would be like in the bedroom. He stirred up a lot of jealousy in introverted, conservative, insensitive men who couldn't be like him, who didn't know what to do with their women. He was handsome, confident, and charming, and he had a lot of natural class and charisma. Men envied him, and women admired him.

Beauty and talent are gifts from God, but sometimes they can be cursed by those who have the Devil in them.

They said that he had died in the hospital during an operation gone wrong. The truth was that the Mafia plotted to kill him because he didn't want to pay them protection money.

Some of their women were seen in his company, but there was nothing they could do to keep their women away from this man who all the women were dreaming of.

When he died, his funeral was as large as the one for Princess Diana. She too died for love and for the sake to defend the most vulnerable.

His life was cut short; he didn't finish what he had come to do. That's why he had to come back.

This time, he did things differently. Now, I leave to you to read it so that you can work out from this chronicle of the story of my life and the connection with other renowned characters who have originated from the spirit of Pan.

His name was Rudolph Valentino.

CHAPTER 1
Nick's Life Story

I was born to a humble, southern Italian family in Capurso, in the province of Bari, in 1961. Growing up on the streets, my childhood was adventurous. In those days, we didn't have computers, Internet, or PlayStation to keep us at home. We invented our own games or played the games that had been handed down by previous generations. Boys often played with marbles, or we'd squash beer bottle tops to play close to the wall, pretending it was real money. I played endless games of soccer.

I was chased numerous times by the security guards in the fields on the outskirts of town where I would go with my school friends to find finch nests and steal grapes, cherries, and other fruits during summertime. In autumn, we'd collect twigs and leftover logs to burn fires so that we could gather around the fire like American Indians to tell each other jokes and old tales passed on by our elderly relatives.

I still miss the air of my native homeland in Italy, the smell of the almond blossom, the robins that no longer return as much as they used to in the springtime. Some of us migrants with our hearts torn between two countries, our souls may never rest in peace in the one place.

My father had always enough work in his trade as a tiler, but there was only one problem: people wouldn't pay at the end of the week. There was a tradition where people would get their jobs done and then pay later whenever they had the money. It was a struggle for him to go from job to job like a gypsy then having to wait to get paid or to get the rest of the money. With all that was owed to him for his work, by the time he paid his workers, he could not make ends meet to support his wife and four children.

My mother Camilla, father Martin, and sister Pia
on my second birthday, 1962.

Sick and tired of the same old routine, he decided to migrate to Switzerland in 1967. Living alone, without his family, he was unable to budget his earnings and save, so he returned home a few months later, empty handed. I can't forget how tough that year was. My mother and I had lined up in front of the municipal council's doorsteps to get some money and a food voucher to feed the family. There were days when all my sisters and I had to eat was chicken soup and pasta or bread and milk.

They were the days of the revolution and the Vietnam War, when university students fought the injustices of the government for human rights and jobs.

From an early age, I liked singing and drawing. I was growing up with the music of The Beatles, Pink Floyd, Lucio Battisti, and Bread. I used to dance near the jukebox in the café at the botanical gardens. I wished on the stars that I could learn English and dreamt of going to Hollywood someday. My primary school teacher, Gino Pastore, and the choir teacher encouraged me to sing. They wouldn't send me home at the end of the day on Friday unless I sang a song of *Canzonissima* in front of the entire school.

My primary school friends until fifth grade before we left Italy.
I'm in the top row, fourth from the left.

In 1968, I was invited to participate in *Io Zecchino D'oro,* the most popular Italian TV young talent-singing quest. My father turned down the offer because he couldn't afford to take me to Bologna. This was the first disappointment of my life and, after it, I stopped singing at parties whenever I was asked. I soon learned that in life, it is a disadvantage to be born into a family who can't help you or refuses to make an effort to help you.

At the age of ten, in 1971, I got my first job working in a pizzeria: fetching logs for the furnace, going up and down the stairs, serving tables, and washing the dishes at the end of the night. I earned $1.50 a week and a pizza and Pepsi to take home every night, and tips if I got to the table to collect the bill before the owner's wife, who often got there first, kept it for herself.

Of all my childhood memories that I recall, one that I cherish dear to my heart is my first (puppy) love: for Francesca Delite. She was a year older than me, and she was already growing to be an attractive young woman. She was a beautiful Mediterranean brunette with olive complexion and dark eyes.

I was a child compared to her, but I was already making ambitious plans to grow up quickly. I couldn't wait to go to high school so that I could propose to her to become my girlfriend. I would meet up with her punctually at the same street corner every morning to walk to school with her, just to spend another moment of my day next to her. I would offer her my Brios snack bars and all I had in my lunchbox.

I used to go to church on Sundays with the excuse to see her, and, if I had any pocket money, I'd offer her a gelato or fried pizza. After school in the afternoon, I'd go up and down her street and whistle until Francesca would come out and ask me to lend her my bike to go for a ride around the block. Girls in those days often wore miniskirts, and I couldn't help but to try to look between her legs every time she went up and down.

She could sense that I was looking at her, so she would stare straight into my eyes. I do believe that she purposely enjoyed opening her legs wider just to tease me. She always used to ring the doorbell whenever she went past my house and would leave a message with my mum: "Tell Nick that Francesca says hello."

In August 1972, the Arborea family migrated to Melbourne, Australia. The night I left Italy was the first time I hugged and kissed Francesca. We promised to keep in touch; I wrote to her, but she never replied. My letters never reached their destination. Her mother or older sister must have read them and thrown them away. She must have thought that I had forgotten her in Australia, but little did she know how much I missed her, how desperately lonely I was in Australia, and how much I was longing to see her.

Receiving (left) the first-prize children's art award from the captain of the Marconi ship on the way to Australia.

Singing (right) "My Sweet Lord" with my sisters and brother. From left: Carmel, myself, Pia, and Vince.

Life in Australia didn't turn out as we had anticipated. When the ship arrived in Perth, it seemed as if we had just landed in paradise. There was a sunny, clear-blue sky as well as palm trees and huge green gardens, and the buildings and homes were just like the ones we had seen in American movies. There were bigger roads and less traffic; everything around was modern. We immediately noticed the difference. I remember telling my parents that if Melbourne was going to be like this, I was going to love living in Australia.

But the worst was yet to come. The weather in Melbourne was unstable, not like it was back home in Italy. Melbourne is winter one day and summer the next. We lived for the first two weeks in a house of family friends before they found us a place to rent.

Within that same week, my father found work in a pipe foundry, pulling hot pipes out of the oven. He could not speak a word of

English, and those who could speak Italian wouldn't give him a break to go to lunch or even the toilet. He was already planning to go back to Italy. Soon though, a family friend found a tile shop that was looking for workers, so within a few days he was back to his tiling job. My mother also found work with LM Ericsson, a telecommunications factory, assembling parts for telephones.

In those days to get a job, you didn't need to be an electrical engineer; they didn't ask you for previous work experience. People were trained on the spot. They were shown, *hands on,* how to do the work. They even sent her to school twice a week to learn English. After a few months, she was already a supervisor and bringing home a better wage than my father.

Petrol and food prices went up every year to pay for a war for petrol and religious differences rather than democracy, to waste 12,000 euros a month to keep an allied soldier in the Middle East. Every morning when my parents left home to go to work at 7.00 a.m., I was left behind to take care of sisters and a little brother, who had just started grade prep. I had to make sure they got neatly dressed, brushed their teeth, had breakfast, and got to school and back safe, and then I watched them until our parents got back from work at 5.00 p.m. I became a victim of bullying so going to school became a nightmare for me. I got picked on at Coburg Technical School because I was a "wog." I found myself in the ring almost every day.

In the 1970s, racism was still alive, especially against Europeans who were fresh off the boat. My first English teacher was an Egyptian who could speak more than one language. He had Italians, Greeks, and Turks all learning under the same roof. He spoke English with a very strong European accent. So much for speech therapy! You'd think that the government, in areas with high densities of migrants would have a proper English teacher, wouldn't you? His accent rubbed off on a lot of those students and, for that reason, after thirty-five years I still speak English with a bit of an accent.

I have come to the conclusion that kids are generally alike, when they are little. As they grow older, they are affected and conditioned by the environment in which they live, because they don't have a choice to escape from it until they are old enough to go on their own.

I have always been an individual, and through high school I had few friends. My best friends became the characters on TV, particularly those from *The Brady Bunch* and *Gilligan's Island,* and also *The Partridge Family* and *I Dream of Jeannie.* I grew up with the Brady kids and had an appointment with them every day. I learned English from them, and they were my role models. I owe a lot of thanks to that sitcom! I also loved to watch *Kung Fu,* taking note of the teaching and discipline that the master taught his student, Grasshopper.

From early 1973, my father started working on his own. Every weekend, and often on Fridays, I had to skip school to give him a hand working as a tiler labourer.

My father was, and is, an aggressive man. Working for him was daunting—not only physically stressing but also mentally exhausting. I had to shovel many mountains of sand and cement for him, while he'd stand there watering it with the hose! I had to cut tiles placed over a toilet seat, with the smell of sewage in my face. All his life, my father has only been good at giving orders and making people do the work for him. He is always negative and ready to contradict everything. He never cared about what I wanted to do with my life. He was only concerned that his oldest son served him. I could never rely on him for moral or financial support.

As my sister Pia would say, we were never raised in a loving, peaceful environment. My father was always a stubborn man who never had a good reason not to trust me and support me when I needed his help. I wanted to leave home many times, but I had nowhere to run. With my nearest relatives 20,000 miles away, where would I go?

Though suppressed and lonely, I didn't lose my passion for art. In year ten, I should have been awarded with the scholarship for art and graphics, but the teachers voted against me because they considered me a rebel. But the opposite was true: I was the one getting beaten up and bullied by the packs of "yobbos."

However, there was one teacher who stood up for me. My art teacher, Mrs. Fishpool, felt sorry for me and gave me an award of her own. She bought me an art book titled *The Dawn of Time* and gave me a cheque for ten dollars—something precious to me which I still treasure today. She was also very attractive, and I could never take my eyes off her.

She wrote in *The Dawn of Time*, "To Nick, for displaying such enthusiasm in the art classes throughout '74. Keep up the good work, Nick, and don't give up trying. S. Fishpool."

The teachers in high school told my parents that I could become a good architect or commercial designer. My father flatly refused. He turned around and asked me to translate for him. Then he said, "I can't afford to send you to university. I need you to come and work with me next year." In 1977, I was forced to drop out of high school to go and work with my father as a tiler. For the next four years, I worked for seven days a week. My wage was fifty dollars a week, enough *pocket money* to go out on the weekend, while my father boasted to family friends, "Nick and I made $1,500 this weekend, something the prime minister doesn't even make in three days."

My high school mates at Coburg Tech.

I wasn't being rewarded for my work. Financially however, I was contributing to the progress of my family's welfare. And it's something that I feel proud about, though at times I feel that I missed out on something during all those years I worked for him. My father promised that he would buy me my first car when I got my licence. For two years, I had to save all my pocket money to buy my first third-hand car: an 850 Sports Fiat.

I began to explore Melbourne's nightlife. Those were the days of *Saturday Night Fever*—the disco era had begun. I was going solo from one nightspot to another in search for a female companion with whom to dance, hoping to find a bit of attention and affection I couldn't get from my parents. They were too busy with their friends and their Italian social club to care and be concerned about their kids. I soon became a regular, notorious face of the Dolce Vita of the Little Italy of Carlton.

Every weekend, I was seen around Melbourne in the company of a new, beautiful girl. While in Hollywood, John Travolta and Richard Gere were making movies about the Latin lovers, I was beginning to live the part of one in reality.

I became a friend to several girls of different migrant backgrounds. I was their toyboy, someone they could show off as a platonic dancing friend. Whenever I didn't have a new date, I would always catch up with the same group of girls: Hanna, Loredana, Voula, and Grace. They were always there for me when I needed them and I was always there whenever they needed me, especially when they used the phrase "catch up," meaning "I need you for sex tonight!" Of the four, those I slept with will remain a secret, just in case someday one of them reads this book, I'd like to keep it private. But they know who they are!

15 July, 1981

Dear Nick,

Hi, how are you? We are all well and hope you are too.

Sorry we haven't written but we have been studying very hard.

(Do you believe us?!!!) Thank you very much for that postcard you wrote us. We didn't expect you would write. We have heard that it's very warm in Rome, more than 30 degrees C. Here we are fr-ee-ee-eezing!

Wish we were there. Have you been to the beach? What are the girls like? Do you miss us? You have told us about your cousin (the blonde with the blue eyes). We would very much like to have a photograph of him. By the way, Notturno's is not worth going to anymore! There are not too many places to go to these days. We very much miss your company. Please write back to us. Tell us what you have been doing and tell us when you are coming back.

Arrivederci
Baci da,
Hanna e Loredana
xxxxxx

Dear Nick,

How are you? We hope to see you again.

We miss the times when you used to take us parking or for a walk in the gardens. Do you still remember?

Grace and Carmen

I often wondered if they ever spoke to each other about me, if they were aware of the game that I was playing. I prayed that I wouldn't get caught. Perhaps they all knew about it and the joke was on me, and I was their puppet on a string. They were all intelligent, career-minded women doing their last year at university. I guess they were all after a good time too and none of them was ready to settle down with the one guy and have a family yet.

Of all the four, I really tried very hard to impress Voula. She was the first woman who had the qualities of everything I was searching for in a woman. I loved her beauty, femininity, style, and finesse. She had lots of natural charm and class. Voula never found an excuse not to go out. She always made time for me. I was falling in love with her, but Voula could only offer me a platonic friendship as she wanted to meet and marry a Greek man.

9/12/83

I've known Nick Arborea for the past six years and in this time he has proven to be one of the most trustworthy friends I have.

He's witty and quick in his replies, full of confidence in his answers, but most importantly shows the extraordinary caring and understating side of his character when one needs his support.

Nick is very punctual in his appointments, especially with women, and he gets along very well with people due to his friendly, happy, easygoing, and caring nature.

Finally, I believe Nick, due to all the qualities I have listed above, shows great potential in a working position involving people.

Yours sincerely
Voula

In 1980, I met another Andria, an Italian girl whose parents came from the same part of Italy as myself. Within a short time of meeting, we had grown attached. Andria loved me and she had all the cards in the right place: she was still a virgin, and she was yearning to be married. She won my heart, but I was still torn between two countries and I wanted to go back home to Italy.

In 1981, I went back to Italy. I wrote to her to tell her that I was coming back. I asked her to wait for me. She didn't wait; she moved on. She wrote back to tell me that she had met another Italian guy called Reno, a hairdresser like her. Today, Andria has a teenage daughter and is divorced from Reno.

3 December 1981

Dear Andria,

I am so happy to have received your letter at a time like this. I didn't write earlier because I didn't have much to tell you.

I have caught up with time and the life in Italy. I speak Italian well now, better than I ever did.

I miss Australia, especially when I hear an English song. The other night when I went out with other soldiers, I heard a new song by a band called The Police: "Roxanne."

For a minute, the sound of that music reminded me of you and those beautiful, sandy, remote, Australian beaches. For a minute, I missed Australia and especially you.

I hope you wait for me till I get this discharged from army service.

I like it here, but there's no guarantee that I'll be staying unless I find a job here. If you love me, you'll stay in touch and be patience.

Warm hugs and kisses with amore (love),

From Sabaudia,

Yours,
Nick.
PS I miss you. Write soon!

Dear Nick,

I was glad to have received a post from you. After such a long time, I had thought you had forgotten me.

Have you settled into Italy yet? It's a beautiful place, isn't it? What do you mean when you say things aren't as you expected?

It hasn't been long since you've been there.

I'm sorry I didn't see you just before you left. I waited for you, but you didn't come. I also had a little gift for you.

I saw your family a few times before they left. We went to a picnic and we spent a bit of the day together. It was a funny day. I wanted to make some coffee so we got a pot and I started to boil water. Oh, it took so long to boil over the barbecue! I dipped my finger into the water to see if it was hot. It felt hot, but when we drank it, it was cold. We had lots of laughs.

How are your sister and your brother? I guess you're happy now that your family is with you. Will you be in Italy forever or will you return to Australia?

How are your studies? You're probably too busy doing other things. I know how easily your mind is distracted.

I'm going out with a very nice guy. His name is Peter. My parents have met him too. We are both happy. Peter used to come to school with me. But we were both afraid to approach each other. Now we have become very close.

I was in a beauty quest 2 weeks ago. Now I'm going to enter in the Miss Victoria quest. It should all be exciting.

My brother Tony is in France now. He will be returning to Italy. You might see him?

I finish school in a month then I will start working. I wish to save enough money so that I can come to Italy—perhaps in three years—if nothing happens.

Well, Nick, I sign off.

Answer my letter soon. Give my regards to your family.

I give you my best wishes,
Andria

In Italy, I tried to find work and ended up in the army for a year. One of the only possibilities to find work there was to try to get into the police force. My uncle had a friend in Rome who could recommend my application. I got called to go for the trials in Rome two weeks before I was discharged from the military service. Unfortunately, the day I was going to Rome, I fractured my foot playing soccer. The medical lieutenant wouldn't allow me go to the police academy. He said he would call them on my behalf, but didn't do it—and as it was the era before mobile phones, I could not call them. I was dismissed by the police academy, and I was asked to enrol in the next recruitment. I was disappointed to have missed out on a career opportunity that would have allowed me to live in Italy.

During the time I was in the army, I met Mary, a girl from my neighbouring town. We liked each other and went out for a pizza a few times. When she wrote to me, she mentioned another man she hadn't told me about. Her parents wanted her to marry him. He was her boss and already had a house and other properties. With me, she would have to go and live in Australia, start a new life, and work together with me to buy our first home. What hope did I have? I stopped writing to her and, when I went back to Bari, I didn't bump into her. She didn't write back to find out why I stopped writing.

10.3.1982

Hello Nick,

I am Mary. Before I begin this brief letter, I would like to thank you for your letter. I have just finished reading it right now so I decided to write.

Unfortunately, my absence from work for family reasons prevented me from reading it. I ask you to forgive me because I am finding it hard to write because I hardly know you, and

because I feel attracted by you after that romantic night we had. I am beginning to feel confused.

However, the first thing I agree to correspond with you and continue our friendship.

Even though, for now my answer is no, you know I am busy with a guy that my parents want me to marry because he's got money and a roof.

I'm having a very difficult time and I'm tired, especially at work. He drains me because I work with him. So for now I want to be free, think a little to myself.

Please accept these few lines of my letter as I'm feeling empty right now. I hope next I feel better. I must leave you now. I'm tired and I need to go to bed.

Let's keep in touch because you've been on my mind and I'm fascinated by you and I want to get to know you better. I loved dancing with you at carnival. You're a great dancer and you seduced me with your charm and elegance. A real gentleman.

It has been a pleasure to have known you, even though it's been very brief.

Til next time,
Love, Mary

During my army service, I also met an American girl named Eva in Rome. I spent a memorable day with her, showing her around. When I returned to Australia, she wrote to me twice but we eventually lost touch.

After leaving the army in 1982, I found myself running out of money, and all my attempts to get a job in Italy failed so I was forced to come back to Australia.

4.4.83

Dear Nick,

Come Stai? I'm so happy and excited to hear from you. I thought after few months come by I wouldn't hear from you.

I would have written to you but I lost your address when I got back to America. I didn't forget how much you've helped me to show me my way around Rome and the unforgettable night we had together.

We both agreed that it would be a passing fling.

I couldn't have been luckier to have found someone as nice as you to help an American who knew no Italian!

After spending two months here, my Italian got pretty good, for my host family knew no English! What an experience. But in all, I've had a fantastic time here.

I wish we could have continued to see each other. But your army and your return to Australia would have made it impossible to keep in touch.

I hope you write again. I'd like to hear from you.

Sincerely, Eva

August 9, 1982

Dear Nick,

I'm sorry I haven't written to you sooner, but my summer has been so hectic. The girl whose home I visited in Italy last summer spent a month with me here and I was very busy showing her the sights. Besides that, I've also been working in a clothing store as a cashier. It's not a bad job, but it gets boring in the summer months because everyone is away instead of shopping.

How is your summer coming along? It must be so hot in Australia at this time. In your next letter, I'd love for you to explain what you're doing. Describe your town. It might seem strange to you, but us Americans are fascinated with Australia—I especially love your accent!

Last weekend I was at the Men At Work concert. They were great. Are they as big in Australia as they are here?

I'll be looking forward to hearing from you again.

Love,
Eva

In 1982, I finally completed my studies by correspondence and got my diploma in architectural and structural drafting.

I applied for any opportunity that came along, but I never got called for an interview. On one occasion, the CES had mistakenly called my brother instead of me to go for a position as a cadet building inspector for the Broadmeadows Council. He got the position. While my brother started a career that I would have loved to have had, I was forced to continue to help my father, without a wage and under the same distressing conditions.

After so many heated arguments, he decided to increase my pocket money to one hundred dollars for seven-days-a-week work. In those days, a minimum tiler's wage was five hundred dollars for five days of work.

Some ask, "Why did you put up with it? Why didn't you leave home?" It's a lot easier said than done! As you read along, you will find that eventually I did end up leaving home, I blame myself for one thing: for not having left home earlier. I should have left at sixteen and never looked back.

In 1983, I went out with Maroline, another beautiful Italian, a Sicilian brunette. Maroline was just happy to catch up with me for a good time. She wasn't ready to settle down with just one man; she was too hot to have only one. I had great sex with her.

I bumped into her again after twenty-five years. Sometimes you can live in the same city, just around the corner from each other, and fate doesn't make you cross paths again, unless one deliberately goes out of 'one's way to search for an old friend.

That morning over a coffee, she confessed that even when she got married, before her children came along, her husband could not impede her to see her old friends. She truly believes that her children changed her life and tamed her. She told me that if it hadn't been for them, she might have been divorced today. Had she and I had stayed together, she would have put me through the same things she put her husband through. She loved him, because he was a very patient, understanding man. He allowed her the space that she needed to grow, without the guarantee that she was not going to leave him for another man. For that reason today, they have a strong bond they will never break.

In 1984, I met Helena, a beautiful Sri Lankan girl. My first black lover and one of the warmest, most sensual, and most feminine females I ever me—one of the best experiences that I will remember the rest of my life.

We were both too busy having a good time and I felt that I was not ready to take this relationship seriously. We were just happy to *catch up* whenever we could, without strings attached. Whenever I called her, she always made herself available for me. When I stopped calling her, she never called me back to find out why I had stopped ringing her.

We let go of each other without an explanation, without a reason. We just drifted apart, as good friends sometimes lose touch without a reason.

I bumped into Helena a few years ago. She had been married to and divorced from two attractive men. One of them was a police officer. She had kids from both men. The oldest daughter was already fifteen at the time. She confessed that throughout the two marriages, she wasn't ready to settle down with just one man and she was still seeing Michael. She had left Michael for me, and she was still seeing Michael during her marriage. Michael was also married. She doesn't know what ever happened to Michael. He just stopped calling and she lost contact with him. We had another fling after all these years, but she needed someone steady, and I wasn't ready to move in with her. I was still healing from my last breakup and my heart couldn't go back to the past.

Soon after Helena came Lina.

I was working for her father's tile shop to try to break away from my father and this was a situation where I didn't want to mix business with pleasure.

She was doing HSC that year and wanted to go to university to become a medical practitioner. I didn't want to disturb her studies. This was one beautiful Italian girl that I regret to have spared.

Lina wrote to me, but I hesitated to take her out. I never gave Lina the opportunity to get to know me. I didn't want to end up working for another father who was going to remind me, "What did you have when you married my daughter?"

I had already been used by my father, but I didn't want to be used by my father-in-law. In the end, when her father found out what was going on between his daughter and me, I didn't get any more work from him and I lost touch with Lina.

21-5-84

Dear Nick,

This letter has probably come as a shock to you, but I felt it necessary to take up my pen to write to you.

I would like to thank you for attending the barbecue for Miss Florence. It didn't turn out as we had previously planned (dancing all night long), but it was most entertaining in my point of view.

I suppose you were bored to tears, but if you'd noticed the dirty looks my cousin Gina gave me, you'd know why I didn't.

It is as clear as crystal to all my kin that I find you most interesting; in fact, I'm very attracted to your fantastic personality (and intriguing looks).

I felt deeply moved that you were curious about me.

You just don't know how profoundly touched I am, for no one has felt that way towards me for a great, long time. I don't know how you feel at present, since you've found out that I'm only an innocent sixteen-year-old who knows very little about the world of love, and would like very much for someone to teach me!

Due to my restricted freedom, it is very hard for us, but I sincerely hope we can see more of each other soon.

I must lay my pen down and go to bed to have sweet dreams.

Lots of Love,
Lina
xxx

20/2/85

Dear Nick,

Guess who? That's right—it's me.

Would you believe it has taken me this long to put pen to paper and write something sensitive?

Thanks a million for the beautifully perfumed roses. They made my day! My reaction was, "Oh, my God!"

Mum almost had and heart attack. Luisa and Claudia teased me all night. Frank thought it was a joke and didn't know what to think. I thought it was absolutely adorable of you. You deserve a big kiss.

Anyhow, how have you been? I've been studying. I'm in form 6 this year—what a toughie it is. I'm not in bed before 11.30. Last night was 1.15 a.m.

But I keep telling myself it's only for a year. (I hope it is anyway!) I rarely go out as a result of it. But I don't really mind as yet.

I've a stack of homework to do, so I'd better lay down my pen.

Lots of warm hugs and kisses
Love Lina

Lina eventually became a doctor and now lives in Perth, in Western Australia. She got married to a South American man, whom she has since divorced. She has a son who lived in Melbourne with his grandparents. I found out about Lina years later when I bumped into her parents.

In 1985, I met Katia after Lina. Katia really tried to make me happy, to love me with all her heart and soul, and to try to make me forget the past. She also had similar problems with her parents. She understood exactly what I was going through. I had a great time with Katia; she was one of the best lover I had known.

She had a heart of gold, but I was still too attached to the past to recognise her love. I will never forget the night we ended up going parking by mistake, in the driveway of the church, next door to the Bundoora Cemetery. We had almost stripped, before a smoke came out of nowhere to split us up. We both opened the doors quickly to get out because we thought the car was on fire. We then realised, when we looked up, that we were about to have sex in front of a large neon cross.

The smoke that came out of the genie bottle between us had nothing to do with the car burning. There was nothing wrong with the car. We both watched the cloud move toward the cemetery. As I remember, it was a clear, starry night, not a cloud in the sky. No wind.

That was a warning that we were about to do the wrong thing on sacred ground. Since that night, nothing has gone right with my life. No matter how I've tried, I feel as if I was cursed by that ghost. Since that night, I had fear, and whenever I wanted to call Katia, something held me back.

I tried to pick up the phone to call her, to find out why she also stopped ringing, but I always ended up putting the telephone down. Something didn't want the two of us to get back together. If only Katia knew what I went through with my life since then.

If there was ever a time when I have sinned, this was probably when I did it, without realising my actions. We were both in a hurry, like two animals in heat, blinded by lust that we didn't see what we had in front of us.

Then, when I finally found the courage to call her, she had moved on. We ended up splitting up because one evening, when I went to pick her up, I arrived at her house on time, but when I beeped the horn she didn't come out. That seemed unusual. Something told me to go to the lake around the corner from her house. I arrived in time to see her get out of another car. She was saying goodbye to another date she had just finished with, and when I drove past she was shocked to see me. She read in my eyes that I was furious. I drove off.

After that day, I didn't call to ask why she was there, nor did she call me to ask why I didn't call.

Dear Nick,

Hi, I'm writing this letter the night I saw you last. I was lying here in my bed, trying to go to sleep. Believe me: I have never tried so hard, but all I can think about is you and me and what we said and did together.

That last day, I wanted to say many things to you, things that always seem to go astray when I'm with you or talking to you by phone. A lot of things I wish I could have said to you, and maybe when it came to doing so was too afraid, because I was scared of the answers you may have given or the ones you would not.

I can always remember you complimenting me and saying how great I was, and me saying how great you were, which I'm sure you needed to hear. Maybe you would have felt more sure of yourself and not as afraid or unsure not for me but for yourself if I did. I'm sorry. I know I'm late in doing so, but let me tell you you're special!

Your eyes and your smile always made me feel warm and very happy. Your eyes especially. When you looked at me, I felt as if you were looking inside the deepest part of me. Your smile, words could never describe.

I could shake you every time you would put yourself down, doubting your abilities and the gifts you would give of yourself.

Never doubt yourself on the things you give. They could never be bad, because they come from you. You always made me feel good and happy.

Sometimes, today I felt being angry with you and yelling at you, saying, "What's wrong? Do I scare you so much?"

I never ever wanted to hurt you. But I knew from the start it would happen like this. I could never hurt you for the world and I think you know that I won't deny that I didn't want it to end, but I pushed hard.

You once said to me if it came to having to fight would I, tried.

But, even now I still don't know if you wanted me or not. One thing I do know is that something will happen between us again one day. I don't know what or when, but I do feel it. (Don't be afraid, I'm not a witch.)

There are so many things that you said to me that confused me and I wasn't sure what you were trying to say. Sometimes I didn't know if you wanted me or if you didn't, but I think maybe you were confused also.

Please don't confuse my feelings for you as a first experience or first love, because I know that it was not. I'm not saying I love you, but I do care for you a lot and I think it would have grown.

I think a lot of times we were both unsure and afraid of each other. There would be times when we would let go and pretend there was nothing to say and do what felt natural to each other.

But as soon as reality and the fear jumped into our minds, we started to doubt again and be cautious, in both what we said and did, to stay safe just in case. But I think maybe more so for you.

I wish that what she and so badly. It hurts me more than you could ever know to see you hurting. When you talked of her, it was like the Devil wouldn't let you go. You were suffocating and all I could do was listen and see the anger of injustice and fear and, most importantly, the mistrust and abuse of your love.

I never hated you talking about her, I just hated for the way she made you feel. She imprisoned you. I think maybe that's why I let go when you wanted me to. Because I knew that you were beginning to feel that way. Not because I did, I honestly know myself and I didn't, but I think because we were becoming too close and it scared you, not me.

The closeness we had in such a short period at first confused me, but that last Saturday, when we went out and were lying on the beach, it just fell into place. I no longer felt scared or confused.

Maybe you sensed it at the same time. I don't know.

I knew then that after that night it was different. I could see far into the future. Just like you would say, it didn't scare me. I felt sure of you.

I won't deny that I don't feel hurt, because I do. I care for you, and I want you.

I didn't want a brother or a first experience. It wasn't a flirtation. When I really think about it and look far ahead, I think I know it would have lasted.

It scares me just to think about it, but it sounds okay. Like you said, the timing wasn't right, or was it?

I know your priorities including other things, but I knew that. I want you to know I would never have jeopardised them, because I know the passion and need inside you to succeed is important. But, you also had to do them yourself. That's why I could never have interfered, because succeeding for you would mean nothing unless you did it yourself.

The peace you talked about that you are seeking is inside you, and you alone can bring it out. It's already there; just let it go. I know it's hard but I honestly believe sometimes you keep yourself trapped in all the bad luck and anger of the past because you're afraid that, maybe without it, you'll be free and you won't have to rely on it to fall back on.

I don't want to be hard, but you have to let go. I don't use excuses.

All I ever wanted was to be there for you. I knew you and the heart you had and the way you felt about yourself and your life the first time I met you. I wasn't listening to what you were saying. I was looking inside you and the way you were saying it. Don't mistake my wanting to know or be with you as pity either.

You hinted at me and I knew, but I wanted more and more to be there.

Sometimes I think maybe you should have been more of a pig and made it easier, but even when you tried to be selfish by saying you were thinking of number one now, you were still gentle and kind, always trying.

If at this stage you're feeling bad, don't. I'm sure this isn't the end. It was going to happen and I wish it hadn't ended. I feel nothing but good thoughts and caring for you and more, but I dare not say.

I wish you were my first and only. I wish you knew me more. Maybe you wouldn't be so afraid. I would have waited. I still would.

But I can't help feeling sad. I don't understand why you so badly wanted me to go. I've tried to find so many excuses and reasons and thought back to the ones you used or gave me, ones that you thought I was feeling. They were never there because I never felt bad being with you. You weren't an excuse for anything. But I could see that even today after everything. You grabbed and shook me and said, "Don't kill me." Please, you won't do anything to me.

Even though I am the stronger one, I knew it would be you who would want to go, not me. I couldn't, and I know I never would.

I could see what was ahead of me for you and me. You said you had things to do. I knew you did, but I wouldn't stand in front of you. I would only stand beside you, and you the same for me.

You said that I was here to show you what it's like to have someone want you, like you wanted her. Did you fear my caring so much? I only gave to you and felt for you what you gave in return to me.

I just don't understand, because I know in my heart I did nothing wrong and neither did you. So why was it wrong?

I know I'm persisting, but it's like someone all of the sudden wanted to close the light on me. You wanting to go back to Italy, or wanting to live in a flat, or finding her would not have changed me because they were things you wanted to do.

But I don't know if this was one of the things you wanted to do. It's like you gave, but as soon as you felt too close you would take back a little by using excuses or talking about her or things that went wrong in the past. Or more badly—doubt yourself and say things that weren't true. You know they were and so did I.

You said, "I want to be by myself. I want to be alone." I don't believe that. When someone is hurting like you are, he doesn't want to be alone because when you are alone thinking of someone, you wish you were with that person.

I know. I've been there. Only I wish I was here.

But again maybe she's an excuse to keep out the world because at the moment you feel safe inside those walls. I know I stayed in mine for 2 years. Don't make the same stupid mistake I did and hang on to something that's not there.

I think maybe we met because you did want to let go and get out of these walls but you didn't expect it to be so good. So you thought it's too much, it's too good, go away and you're back to that safe place.

But it's not safe. Look inside you and outside of you, how you are feeling. You're not safe because you want to stay in the dark and not come out to the light.

Don't use the things that go wrong as excuses and the things that aren't the way you want as obstacles.

Thinking of you,
Katia

In 1985 after Katia, I met the first Jessica, a sweet Tasmanian blonde. In years to come, there were two other Jessicas. One was a teacher, with whom I went out a few times, and when I bumped into her years later, she told me she was studying to become a film producer. With the third Jessica, our friendship has dragged along over the years and we still keep in touch today.

Jessica from Tasmania really liked me, but I wasn't ready to start another relationship after Jessica. I saw Jessica again at the end of 1986 at a bad time, after I had just split up with first the love of my life, Cassandra. I was too devastated and it was much too early for me to start another relationship with any girl.

6th January, 1985

Dearest Nick

Thank you for the cute Christmas card.

I hope you and your family had a lovely Christmas Eve. I think of you often and wonder what you're doing. I hope you're having much better weather than we are. We had one really hot day here and I went to the beach and ended up rather burned, but because the weather has been cold since I've been covered up and all my skin is starting to peel.

I let you have quite a tan by now and, although I'd rather have your weather, I'd much rather have our beaches. We have simply gorgeous beaches down here!

My sister and I spent this last weekend camping up at Strahan (which is on the west coast) and practically got washed away because the weather was so wild and rough.

I'm back at work of course and still at my sister's.

Keep well and stay sexy!

Love and best wishes,
Jessica
xoxo

2nd May, 1985

Darling Nick,

I hope you are in good health and good spirits.

I am wondering why I have not heard from you since talking to you on the phone at work and of course since receiving the most beautiful rose in the world from the most handsome Italian stallion I know.

I have sent this to your home address, even though you asked me not to, because you have not notified me your new address. So I sincerely hope you receive this all right.

What are you doing with yourself employment-wise? Work for me is fine at the moment.

I am travelling to Switzerland with my family in a fortnight for 14 days on the gold coast at my father's expense. I am really looking forward to it.

Naturally I understand that there would be many new ladies in your life, and by writing this letter I am not trying to renew a claim on you. But this is just a note to let you know how much I loved and appreciated your St. Valentine's Day gift and I hope your dreams are slowly becoming reality. I shall be truly ecstatic if you were to send me a line or two on the state of your well-being at present.

Love,
Jessica

Dear Nick,

The hotel is in Elizabeth St. And if you keep following it down you will come to the city centre.

Buses run fairly regularly! I expect to be home by 4.15 p.m. and I have lunch at 12.30. Work n . . . .

Have a nice day. See you soon.

Jessica

In 1985, I also met Susan, a blue-eyed Italian, Venetian beauty who was runner-up at the Miss Italy beauty pageant, with my sister Carmela, but Susan was a bit short-fused and temperamental. She was impatient and feared losing me.

One night she had one of her lunatic mood swings because I was running late for our appointment. She slammed the phone in my face and didn't even give me the chance to explain. I really liked Susan, but I didn't call her back to find out what got into her that night. Neither did she call me to find out why I stopped calling.

1-4-1985

Meeting you Nick, has been like finding the last piece of a puzzle.

Something you know will complete the picture; make it come to life again.

Despite the fact we've only known each other for a short while, I feel I've known you all my life, that I knew you existed, that you were wandering around there, but I couldn't go out and look for you. It had to happen by itself as a natural attraction by soul mates.

I honestly believe it was more than a coincidence. Listening and talking to you, more and more, I see ourselves as very similar people.

I always knew there was someone out there who was very much like me, but I never thought I'd meet him. But I have, and it feels very nice, very comforting, and exciting.

I have a premonition that our meeting each other is going to create something very good for us, and it will. I only hope that you won't disappoint me, Nick. Please don't hurt or use me, because this I fear more than anything else.

I can only respect and cherish you, hoping you'll do the same—well, only time will tell us, I suppose. Faithfulness has disappointed me in the past, and I still believe in it, so I hope to find it in you.

I tell you these things with all my heart and soul because I know you understand. I'd like us to grow closer and fonder of each other because I know we can be good together.

If you feel the way I do about you, we will fulfil our desires together—you'll see.

—Susan

In 1986, at twenty-five years of age, I finally left home for the first time and went to live on my own in a city, which I still couldn't call home. Within a few days, I met Cassandra. She became the first girlfriend who moved in with me.

She was Greek and had similar problems with her parents as I had with mine. We were both Leos and we had too much in common; we were like twins. She was the female version of me. We had found love in each other, but we didn't have the financial security. Love was not enough to keep us together.

We tried to get a fashion label off the ground. It was called Italmode. We ended up mixing business with pleasure and when things didn't turn out to our expectations, she didn't stand by me. At the time, with the money we had, we could have opened our first boutique. Instead, I trusted her advice, because she was a manager for Myer's sunglasses department. I was persuaded to our own production.

She dumped me for the manager of a hotel where she worked part-time until three in the morning, on the thirty-fifth floor of the old Regent, now the Sofitel Hotel.

19.2.1985

Dear Nick,

I came to see you today, but I guess luck, wasn't with me.

Anyway I won't let that stop me. We'll try again on Friday. Maybe we can go out this weekend.

Meanwhile I hope you're keeping well and not eating more than just burned rice.

We'll see you very soon.
Cassandra

My Dear Friend Nicola,

Hope you approve of my spring cleaning. Thought you might like to feel a touch of spring today, especially since you likened today's weather with that of a typical spring day in Italy.

I wish you and your family a peaceful and Happy Easter.

Keep smiling.

See you soon.
Cassandra

Dear Nick,

I'm very sorry about tonight. I tried to contact you to let you know but I couldn't. The Victoria Hotel called me at work to ask if I could help in the main cocktail bar, tonight at 6 p.m.

I forgot we were going to my parents'. I hope you will forgive me.

I got a medical certificate from a doctor today so I won't be working Thursday and Friday. Please visit them with me tomorrow. PTO.

I bought a video tape today. It's on the table. Go inside the flat and get it. You know where the key is. Please, please, please tape Richard Gere for me tonight at 8.30 p.m.? *Breathless.*

My favourite Film!

Love, Cassandra

PS I finish work at 10.30 p.m. tonight. We can go for a coffee if you want to meet me at work.

In 1986, I also met the winners of the 1982 soccer World Cup, Paolo Rossi and friends, on their club Italia tour in Australia. I was their guide to show them around Melbourne.

This was the first time in my life that I rubbed shoulders with some famous people. They gave me the opportunity to warm up with them before the game at the Olympic Park. All the people and friends who knew me from Lygon Street cheered my name loudly from the crowd.

In that moment, I had my five minutes of fame. I played so well that my very best performance came out of me. One of the managers, Claudio Sala, was so impressed with me that he invited me to go back to Italy with them to try out with Prato, a C division I club that was trying to get promoted to Series B. But I had no money to go there to see if I could make the team and get a contract.

That weekend, I had to borrow three hundred dollars from my sister Pia just to have enough money in my wallet to be among them.

I was too embarrassed to tell Mr. Sala that I was broke and penniless and didn't have anyone to borrow money from to go to Italy. I should have told him the truth that I was a tiler and still working for my father. He probably would have offered to help me out until I got the contract, which would then have enabled me to pay him back.

I should have believed in myself and swallowed my shame and pride. I found the excuse that I had business commitments and couldn't go. I felt devastated for not being able to seize the opportunity of a lifetime.

I took it as another one of those things in life that wasn't meant to be.

In 1987 came Julie . . . this one was no Giuliette! Another short-lived love story that for a moment made me believe in love again. This was a story that I had to forget.

This girl had more than two feet in one shoe.

Julie had the beauty of a true Mediterranean goddess. She was stunning—dark-skinned with olive eyes. There was something mysterious about this girl, but I never managed to find out.

In 1987, I also met the Pugliese delegation of the Italian state government on their tour to Australia. At the time, I was working casually as a security guard, so I assisted them on their trip to Adelaide and Sydney as their security guard and interpreter.

Six months later, I was invited to go to Italy as group leader of the Young Italians Cultural Group. I was also a representative and observer of the Pugliese of Australia. For a short period, I was a correspondent to their monthly migrant magazine. I made some contacts that I had hoped would bring me a business proposition and enable me to start a business bridge that would allow me to travel to Italy for work. But nothing eventuated!

When I was in Italy, Julie wrote to me, but she didn't mean any of those words. When I returned, one night, when we were supposed to go out together, she called me to postpone the appointment. When I put the phone down, I decided to go and pick her up from work. When I arrived there, I saw her walking toward the car with a black guy. I didn't need to see anymore. From that night onward, I just wanted to forget I ever met her.

9.11.87

Tell me what it is that makes us feel that we are friends.

Even though we don't know each other yet . . .

Tell me what it is that makes us feel so united as one,

Even though we are so far apart . . .

Tell me what is that makes my heart beat so strong,

Deep down . . .

That takes my breath away

And talks to me about love?

If this is truly . . . real love . . . you'll be mine for all my life . . . really mine without a doubt.

If it's not love, you'll remain just a friend.

But just in case under this wonderful friendship there's love, what do we do?

Don't do anything, just feel my heart, lost in this great feeling that was supposed to blossom, grow, and stay with us two forever.

Or else forget it. Don't think about anymore about this friendship.

But if this is the way out, maybe, in a year or so, or a century from now, we'll think about this love again . . . that we missed out.

So, leave it like that . . .

Or try to taste this love?

Tell me.

The choice is yours. It's in your hands.

A kiss or two with lots of love.

See you for now and think about this proposal.

My life is not a toy that you can put down when you get tired of it. Think well; it's your life too. I will be waiting for your answer. When you've decided, I'll be here waiting.

But if I don't hear your voice in a couple of days, I'll know that it wasn't love and remember that I have to decide too even though I haven't thought about anybody else but you.

The choice can be difficult when we talk about two people and the choice that has to be made. Remember that if you go, I'll be missing you.

Julie

In 1988, I met Elisa on a trip to Sydney. She wrote to me, but we never had the opportunity to catch up. We kept in touch by telephone, but eventually we lost touch.

She became a tour operator and started to travel. The last time I called to find out how she was, her mother told me she was getting married in Greece.

Dear Nick,

Late at night I'm still thinking of you and the wonderful impression you've left upon me. You're constantly on my mind, driving me crazy.

I wish I could pick up and go to Melbourne to spend some time getting to know you better. You trapped me with your charm, your style, your beautiful smile; your life is moving so fast and everything seems exciting.

I really believe that you have the power to make things happen in your life, so I know you'll be a success in anything you want to do.

Although our encounter was very brief, you had all the right looks, said all the right things, and made all the right moves to ensure that I'll find it very hard to forget you.

Thank you for the lovely flowers and the time you've spent with me.

You touched my heart.

Thinking of you,

Love,
Elisa

Between 1986 and 1990, I had casual jobs, odd tiling jobs. At one stage, I was forced to wash dishes for an Italian restaurant and depended on Centrelink benefits to survive and make ends meet. I was too shy and embarrassed to be seen on the floor serving people who knew me.

During those difficult years I tried to pursue my American dream.

In 1988, I wrote the jingle for a TV spot for Pino Sylvestre aftershave. I began to write songs, novels, and concepts for new movies.

In 1990, I joined a casting agency (Vision) and made several appearances as a film extra, and I appeared in two local movies as well as commercials and corporate videos. ABC TV's Embassy series *Good Men Die Last* and the international release of *The Heartbreak Kid* contributed to gaining some production experience in front of and behind the cameras. I also worked as a volunteer radio announcer, promoter, and journalist for a migrant magazine. For my first song, *Goodbye '60s,* I received good feedback from reviewers and radio stations. Music from the '60s was making a comeback at the time. However, none of them went out of their way to give me airplay or recommend me to a record company that would release it.

Without a contract of distribution, no song or movie can make money, and your Hollywood dream could remain locked in the drawer. The Beatles were right when they said in life you can't get by without a little help from your friends.

The song *American Pie* was a statement—no, a prediction—made by a musician in the '70s who anticipated that the real music would die. Teenagers today are being fed with a transgressive trend of music and fashion that promotes the use of drugs, violence, and bad attitudes.

Nick Arborea

There are fewer meaningful songs that have a message that make you think and feel good these days.

Kids are being influenced to become hard and insensitive, and that's not cool at all according to me.

13th December, 1988.

Mr. N. Arborea,
4/566 Pascoe Vale Road,
PASCOE VALE, VIC.   3044.

Dear Nick,

Thankyou for your tape and phone call.

After listening to your tape a few times, many of the staff at 3TT thought the song was catchy.

In fact quite a few were singing along.

As pointed out to you, you will have to get a recording contract or release your own independant single to get regular air play.

I wish you all the best with your recording pursuits.

Yours sincerely,

DAVID DALKIN
Programme Director.
Encl:Tape.

AUSMUSIC

AUSTRALIAN
MUSIC DAY

27 November '93
Supporting International Year
of Indigenous People

Head Office
PO Box 307
Port Melbourne VIC 3207
62-74 Pickles Street
South Melbourne VIC 3205
Tel: 03/ 696-2422
Fax: 03/ 696-2979

New South Wales
Marcella McAdam
325 Glebe Point Road
Glebe NSW 2037
Tel: 02/ 552-3232
Fax: 02/ 552-4529

Queensland
Jacinta Brondgeest
PO Box 963
Fortitude Valley QLD 4006
60 Berwick Street
Fortitude Valley QLD 4006
Tel: 07/ 852-2283
Fax: 07/ 852-2296

South Australia
SA Rock Generation
Warwick Cheatle
Fremont Campus
Palmer Road
Elizabeth Park SA 5113
Tel: 08/ 287-1619
Fax: 08/ 287-0136

Tasmania
Anna Waters
Suite 32A
Yorktown Square
Launceston TAS 7250
Tel: 003/ 344-163
Fax: 003/ 313-636

Western Australia
Vicki Caulfield
123 Claisebrook Road
Perth WA 6000
Tel: 09/ 227-7962
Fax: 09/ 227-7897

ACT
Lyn O'Brien
PO Box 424
Civic Square ACT 2068
Tel: 06/ 248-0911
Fax: 06/ 247-7739

Northern Territory
Tony Joyce
11 Stokes Street
Parap NT 0820
Tel: 089/ 817-555
Fax: 089/ 817-555

23rd September 1993

Nic Aborea
157 West Street
Glenroy 3046

Dear Nic,

Thank you for your application to the AUSMUSIC Fresh Tracks demo distribution program.

Your application was assessed and your tape listened to by industry operatives and AUSMUSIC panelists.

Unfortunately, your application has been unsuccessful on this occasion but do use the following feedback below to re-apply.

The production quality of the material is very impressive. Performance quality is quite good, both the musicianship and the vocals. The songs have a strong quality about them.

Once again thank you for applying, and good luck with your music!

Yours sincerely

Tony Campbell
Fresh Tracks Manager

AUSTRALIAN CONTEMPORARY MUSIC DEVELOPMENT COMPANY LIMITED
A.C.N. 008 040 902

The record industry is not difficult; it's the bureaucrats who control the industry who can't tell the difference between a good song and a bad one that makes it impossible for newcomers with decent songs to compete.

How will there be room for new songs when radio stations stick to the old ones? We've heard them all for thirty years, and many of the artists are now dead. Those artists who are still alive, struggling for radio airplay and promotion, could afford to retire on the proceeds of their royalties.

It's also unclear how they can justify that a remake of an old song sells better than a good new song that the world hasn't heard yet. If the original on 45 and CD sounds better, why on earth would I go and buy a remake? Record producers, A & R managers, and radio stations have no excuse to why they can't make space for new talent with decent, fresh tracks.

In 1988 also came Diana. She had been with her boyfriend for six years, but threw the relationship away to come and have sex with me twice a week. I persuaded her to go back to him. We were together for three months. She dumped me on my birthday, as a birthday gift.

Dear Nick,

I hope you're not going to feel deserted, but I don't think there's any point dancing around the subject.

All my life I followed my feeling, which is usually right. That's why I left my boyfriend for you.

I've got to go my own way, and I hope you'll understand. Even though I feel a certain attachment to you, I can continue in this way.

I'll always think of you as a friend and a great lover and remember the love that we knew. Deep down, I know God has different plans for us.

Love,
Diana

Ps Have a good time on your birthday, regardless of me. Don't let me get you down. No one's worth that xxx.

I didn't let Diana upset me and that weekend, in Carlton, I met Jennifer, who made up for what I had missed on my birthday. Jennifer was freshly divorced, but I didn't want to use and abuse her generosity. She came from an Italian, honoured family. Jennifer was attractive, warm, erotic, and would have made a good Italian wife. I had to watch out with this one, because if her brothers found out, they could have mobbed me, or made me an offer that would have been difficult to refuse.

We Can't . . . But God Can!

Why things happen as they do, we do not always know, and we cannot always fathom

Why our spirits sink so low . . .

We flounder in our dark distress. We are wavering and unstable, but when we are most inadequate the lord God's always able . . .

For though we are incapable, only God is powerful and great and there's no darkness of the mind that God can't penetrate . . .

And all that is required of us whenever things go wrong is to trust in God implicitly, with a faith that is deep and strong.

And while he may not instantly unravel all the strands of the tangled thoughts that trouble us, he completely understands, and in his time we have faith. He'll gradually restore the brightness to our spirit that we've been longing for . . .

So remember there's no cloud too dark for God's light to penetrate if we keep on believing and have faith enough to wait!

I Want to Help

Is there anything I can say to make you not hurt so much today?
I see you're upset
And I feel it too—deep inside.
I'm helpless, but I want so much to help.
Can I say anything or do anything?
I wish I had the answer you need to hear.
I'm trying . . . but I guess that's the most I can offer for now.
It's an ear to listen and, even more,
An open heart so you'll know that I care and you'll know
that I'm always here.

Don't Ever

Don't ever try to understand everything.
Some things will just never make sense.
Don't ever be reluctant to show your feelings when you're happy; give into them!
Don't ever be afraid to try to make things better; you might be surprised at the result.
Don't ever take the weight of the world on your shoulders.
Don't ever feel frightened of the future.
Take life one day at time.
Don't ever feel guilty about the past—

What's done is done.
Learn from any mistakes you might have made.
Don't ever feel you're alone . . .
There's always somebody to reach out to.
Don't ever forget that you can achieve
So many of the things you can imagine—
Imagine that! It's not as hard as it seems.
Don't ever stop loving!
Don't ever stop believing!
Don't ever stop dreaming your dreams!

Take the Bitter and the Sweet to Make a Life Full and Complete

Life is a mixture,
Of sunshine and rain,
Laughter and teardrops,
Pleasure and pain.

Low and high tides,
Mountains and pains,
Triumphs and defeats,
And loses and gains.

But always in all ways,
God's guiding and leading
And he alone knows
The things we're most needing

And when he sends sorrow
Or some dreaded affliction,
Be assured that it comes
With God's kind benediction.

And if we accept it
As a gift of his love,
We'll be showered with blessings,
You and father above.

A Friend Is a Gift of God

Among the great and glorious gifts
Our heavenly father sends
Is the gift of understanding
That we find in loving friends.

You in this world of trouble,
That is filled with anxious cares
Everybody needs a friend
In whom they're free to share

The little secret heartaches.
That lie heavy on their mind,
Not just a mere acquaintance
But someone who's just our kind.

For somehow in the generous heart
Of a loving, faithful friend
The good God in his charity
And wisdom always sends

A sense of understanding
And the power of perception
And mixes these fine qualities with kindness
And affection.

So when we need someone's sympathy
Or a friendly hand to touch,

Or an ear that listens tenderly
And speaks words that mean so much.

We seek our true and trusted friends in the knowledge that
we'll find
A heart that's sympathetic and an understanding mind . . .

And often just without a word
That seems to be a union
Of thoughts and kindred feelings for God
Gives true friends communion.

Nick,

I know this poem wouldn't seem entirely appropriate in your
eyes,

Seeing that we have just recently met, but there is a lot of
truth in it.

I honestly feel as if I've known you for much longer, because
of your warmth and beautiful qualities that flow out of you
so naturally.

God has certainly bestowed you with a wonderful gift. And
I am grateful that we have met.

I would be so proud and happy to have you as a true friend
for a long time to come, hoping the feeling in mutual.

The Gift of Friendship

Friendship is a priceless gift that cannot be bought or sold.
But its value is far greater than a mountain made of gold.

For gold is cold and lifeless,
It can neither see not hear,
And in the time of trouble
It's powerless to cheer.
It has no cars to listen,
No heart to understand,
It cannot bring you comfort
Or reach out a helping hand.
So when you ask God for a gift,
Be thankful if he sends
Not diamonds, pearls, or riches,
But the love of a real, true friend.

Let Go and Let God

When you're troubled and worried and sick at heart
And your plans are upset and your world falls apart,
Remember God's ready and waiting to share
The burden you find much too heavy to bear.
So with faith, let go and let God lead the way
Into a brighter and less troubled day.

Be Good Cheer, There's Nothing to Fear

Cheerful thought like sunbeams lighten up
The darkest fears for when the heart is happy
There's just no time for tears.
And when you're "high-spirited"
You cannot feel low down
For the nature of our attitude
Toward circumstantial things
Determines our acceptance
Of the problems that life brings
And since fear and dread and worry

Cannot help in any way,
It's much healthier and happier to be cheerful every day.
And if you'll only try it,
You'll find, without a doubt,
A cheerful attitude's something
No one should be without.
For when the heart is cheerful,
It cannot be filled with fear.
And without fear the way ahead
Seems more distinct and clear.
And we realize there's nothing
We need ever face alone
Our heavenly father loves us
And our problems are his own

It's a Wonderful World

In spite of the fact we complain and lament
And view this old world with much discontent
Deploring conditions and grumbling because
There's so much injustice
And so many flaws,
It's a wonderful world
And it's people like you
Who make it that way
By the things that they do.
For a warm, ready smile
Or a kind thoughtful deed,
Or a hand outstretched
In an hour on need
Can change our whole outlook
And make the world bright
Where a minute before
Just nothing seemed right.
It's a wonderful world

And it always will be
If we keep our eyes open
And focused to see
The wonderful things
Man is capable of
When he opens his heart
To God and his love.

My dear friend Nick,

Hoping with all my heart that these inspirational verses will inspire you the way they do me. Whenever you're feeling down and your cares are too much to bear, do as I do. Go over these poems and you'll find as I do that the cross we are bearing isn't as heavy as it seems.

Hoping you will appreciate them enough to give you faith, strength, patience, more wisdom, and a sense of realizing that things are not as bad as they seem.

And most of all, hoping they'll bring you a warm, wonderful feeling of happiness as you read, because they certainly affect me to that extent. Hoping it will for you too.

I know you're not perfect, because nobody is, but believe me when I say if people had more beauty within themselves, as you do, it would be a wonderful world to live in.

Dear Nick,

Wishing you a warm and wonderful Christmas and a new year filled with prosperity.

I sincerely hope that 1989 will have for you many wonderful, exciting things, and may it be a year of collecting your most desired dreams.

I wish you all these things as a genuine friend from within the depth of my heart. My brother John was absolutely right when he said, "You're a top guy!"

Once again all the best for the festive season, and may it be a good and safe one for you.

From one St. Nicholas to another.

I can't pass up a bit of humour, ha ha!

Actually, purely from a true, sincere friend, hoping you'll consider me as such.

Love and best of wishes always,
From Jennifer xxx

During the week of my birthday of 1988, I also met Lisa, but I never thought I would hear from her, after that coffee and chat!

To my surprise, I found a note under the door of my flat dated 16 August, 1988, five days after my birthday. My twenty-eighth birthday brought me two women in one week, after being dumped by Diana.

Danni was gorgeous, one of the most beautiful women I've ever met. Feminine, sensual, sexy, one of those who is any man's dream.

She had been a top model in the '80s and was part of a rock band, which was about to get off the ground, when her marriage fell apart.

Elisabeth had three children, to two different husbands, and needed a man to love her children and provide financial support. It didn't take long for her to fall in love with me, and when she proposed to me, I told her I needed time to think about it, because I had to love her and she came with a package.

Two weeks later I made up my mind: it would be okay to give it a try. I was missing her but when I went and knocked on her door, she told me to go away and didn't open the door. She didn't give me a chance to explain. She said, "Go away. You men are all the same. You all judge me, because of my children."

Eventually we remained friends, but by then she had already moved on with other men. I was still available. There was one time after I had split up with Mary Ann, who was also in a rocky relationship, that while her children were at school, we had great sex. But the fun stopped when she told me that a plasterer, who was younger than me, exactly ten years younger than her, was about to move in with her.

Since I lost touch with D, I bumped into her and we had lunch when she was working for Harry, my drafting teacher. Since then, I never saw her again and we eventually lost touch.

16th August, 1988

Hello Gorgeous,

I am sitting here trying to work and I have warm feelings inside thinking of you.

I picture your face smiling so handsomely down over me. Your presence is near. I cannot help smiling when my thoughts are returning of your room and our long discussions, together.

In my silence, you're there with me, and in my waking moments I hug the pillow trying to recapture my memory of

your naked body pressed to mine in harmony. (Of course the pillow is no compensation!!)

I look forward to the next time we meet.

Your ever truly,
Danni

From 1987 to 1989, I lived back home and for two more years I continued to work with my dad. By then I had managed to save enough money to buy my first property. I decided then that it was time to make the switch from tiler to builder.

In 1989 came Frances, a stunning English flight attendant—a true *English rose.* I had the best St. Valentine's a man could ever have.

10th March, 1989

Dear Nick,

Well, sorry I didn't write you sooner. Did you think I'd forget?

After the overnight bus to Sydney—it took me another two whole days to get home! The problem was with the cranky old plane, which meant we had to stop over a t couple of places for the night.

I was knackered when I got home!!

Well, I must thank you for giving me such a lovely evening before I left—I really had a good time.

You know I didn't have any money. Well, I couldn't even afford to pay the departure tax at the airport. They were furious with me, and I had to sign a declaration promising to send that money when I arrived in the UK.

Have you had any luck with all your ideas for designs plus songs, etc? I hope so.

Since I've been home, I've been working hard to pay off my debts—what a drag!

However, I've decided to return to Australia quite soon as I am going to college in September and I'll have to stick around for a while once I've committed myself to studying. I doubt if I'll go to Melbourne for long as I'd see the rest of Australia.

Will you be going to Italy again soon?

My friend is going there in Easter to visit a boyfriend. I'm tempted to go but I've been invited to Germany so I think I'll go there.

Tonight I'm off to get drunk after a hard week's work! I think I deserve it.

I don't know what else to write so I don't want to bore you anymore.

Maybe see you again when I go to Oz.

Bye for now,
Love, Frances x

I got my builder's licence, but I didn't have enough money. The bank would not lend me the full amount to purchase the property. I turned to my father for help for a guarantor signature, but once again he turned me down and refused to give me a lending hand.

So I got involved with Campanelli, a hardworking plasterer who I later discovered had little business sense. The renovation took too long and we ended up spending more than the expected budget. I had no choice but to agree with his wrong decisions, whether I liked them or not.

To top it off, the real estate market also dropped dramatically. There was a market crash in 1989, devaluing any possible chance of making a profit.

A property that was worth between $200,000 and $220,000 we ended up selling for $167,000. By the time the estate agent took his fee, we were left with no money.

That year was one of the worst and most distressing of my life. I lost six months of hard work and $1,200 per month for almost one year before we were able to sell it. After that failure, I lost the will to do and the joy to vivre.

I put this down to experience as doing the right thing with the wrong partner at the wrong time. This was the third time that luck and timing were not on my side.

Had my father helped me, things may have been different. If I had done things my way and been able to make my first monies in 1989, today I would have been in a very comfortable position financially.

After that experience, I was left exhausted. All I wanted to do was fall asleep and die. In 1990, I met Mary who was six years older than me. She took me away with her to Fraser Island to try to help me forget. There, on the beach, we met George Harrison, of The Beatles, one of my favourite childhood idols. But it happened unexpectedly and we didn't have a camera with us. I was just happy to have exchanged a few words with him.

For four and half years, I was Mary's toy boy. Maryann was honest with me and never promised that our relationship would last forever. She warned me that once she hit forty, one night she would stop calling me and that was going to be the sign that it was time to move on.

She had very influential friends who envied the fun she had with me. But they wanted to see her settle down with a professional of her age or older, not some struggling tiler who had failed to succeed.

Dear Nick,

Happy, happy birthday.

Life is just beginning for you now. I wish you all the love, happiness, and best things in life, my friend. You certainly deserve them.

I thought about phoning you, often, but I knew it would only make me miserable, and maybe make you miserable.

When time has healed, perhaps we can be friends. I value your friendship more than anything. You were a part of me for three years, and I believe you truly understood me and I understood you too (though you many deny that).

I needed a partner in life who was motivated, not someone who was knocked constantly by life. To tell you the truth, Nick, I think I will be on my own for the rest of my life. Sometimes it scares me, but it also fascinates me. It means I will be constantly growing, and sometimes when one is in a relationship, you stop growing.

If you haven't met that special lady yet, I pray that you meet her soon. You need to be loved and adored. (That's what keeps you alive.)

I thank you for all the wonderful times we had together (I miss our walks by the river) and the lovely, warm cuddles at night—I really miss your warmth. How couldn't I?

I'm really not carved of stone, but I think my heart is. I closed that off a long, long time ago. I see your beautiful, beautiful face now and I feel sad, Nikita—how you hated that name.

You're right Nick, you don't like Australia—you're Italian and I don't think you'll find happiness in Australia. You need the warm sun on your back; that will make you smile and feel free and happy.

I often think of Cyprus. Perhaps one day I'll go and live there.

Be happy, Nick, and I hope to see you when you're ready to see me for a coffee and a chat.

Every moment of your life is infinitely creative and the universe is endless, beautiful.

Just put forth

A clear enough request

And everything

Your heart desires

Must come to you.

Love, Ann

Does my boyfriend look
_____ ?
Mysterious ? ← ANSWER
Sinister ?

I don't know him
very well, that's why
or else I'll say
he looks cheeky.
(Please turn over).

Sometimes he makes you happy

Sometimes he makes you sad.

Sometimes he makes your day

So you see, he's not that bad.

Your eyes are brown
You have a flair
Your body is sexy.
When it is bare

Your mind is devious
But your heart is true
This must be why
He will always love you.

In 1991, I did some soul searching and started my spiritual journey. I let go of all my ambitions and material pursuits. I learned to meditate every Thursday and Saturday night when I went to an ashram in Fitzroy. For nine years, I did meditation. After I split up from Maryann, between 1991 to 1995, came a string of short relationships.

In 1994, I met Anastasia, a Russian model who invited me to go to Perth. So I decided that it was time to change my life and try my luck elsewhere.

11.4.94

Hello Dear Nick,

This is Anastassia. I have received your letter today. Thank you.

It was very interesting to read it. I like your photograph. I think you're very good looking.

Nick, from your letter I've understood that you want to come to Perth. Perth is very clean and a pleasant town and the ocean is warmer than in Sydney or Melbourne.

It's quite relaxing in here. I live 5 minutes' walk to the beach, 8 minutes to the train station and shops!

I really like and the rent is very cheap. I'm paying only 70 $ p.w. for one bedroom. In this area where I live is very easy to find a place like mine.

When you come here, I've understood you need a place where to stay. I spoke to my mum about you. She doesn't mind if you stay at my place for a few days until I help you to find a place.

I'm sending you my card just in case. Everything else I will tell you about me when I see you. All I want to say is that I live to have a nice and kind friend who I can relax and trust.

I am sorry for my English mistakes. My English is very good but not the best.

Waiting for your reply,
Love, Anastassia xxxx

She was paying too much rent and she could have been paying off her own place. I told her what to do to get a loan. She called me to thank me, a few weeks later, because the bank had lent her the money to buy a flat across from the beach. Whatever she did with it, I am sure that today she would be grateful to have bought it.

For the first three days after I arrived, she left me in her flat on my own while she went to work. When she got home, she wouldn't allow me to take her out for dinner or a coffee, and she had her mother sleeping over every night.

A Russian friend of theirs came to visit, and I learned he was an Olympic kickboxing champion. They spoke in Russian to each other and I could not understand. I became suspicious and decided to pack my bags, leaving her the keys and a note with her mother and left to go to Fremantle. I called her to let her know which hotel I was staying in, but she didn't come.

I found an Italian builder who was ready to give me some units to tile. Had we been able to get to know each other, there was a good possibility that I might have settled in Perth. After two weeks in Fremantle, I came back to Melbourne.

I met Luise, a stunning brunette, in 1995. She had the body of Elle Macpherson and the breasts of a Brazilian goddess. She was a cross between a Chilean father and an Australian mother. She was an intensive care nurse. She called me over on the weekend, only for sex. I would have loved to be with her, but she left me to go to America to find her American Indian chief. Some medium had brainwashed her into believing that her soul mate was a shaman master from Arizona.

Dearest Nick,

Before I leave to go to the USA, I want you to know that even though I never allowed myself to get involved with you emotionally, sexually you've been the most pleasing lover I've ever known so far in my life. You certainly know how to please a woman in that spot.

Thank you for being there for me when I needed you. I am going to miss the pleasure and comfort you gave me when I needed to unwind.

But I have to move on and follow my journey. I'll keep in touch.

**With warm hugs and love,
Yours, Luise.**

After Luise came Marie. I really loved this one. She was another stunner, but this one was from Mauritian parents. I would have loved to introduce her to my family, but she wasn't family-orientated. She came from a broken home with a complex mother she hardly ever saw, and she had no relations in Australia to turn to. She had a bit of a drinking problem and could not relax. She had skolled a bottle of red wine. I tried to introduce her to my sisters, but she always refused to go to their place for dinner. I really loved her but she didn't let me help her.

Dear Nick,

I know how much you love and adore me.

I am sorry that I can't relax and get excited if I don't have a glass or two of red wine. I know how much you hate it when I end up drinking the whole bottle. But that's how I am. I can't help it. I enjoy your company and having sex with you.

You know exactly what ticks me down there. No other man before you has had the patience and the endurance to last the distance with me. You are a top lover, a warm blanket for winter, and a friend that cares—one that I can trust to rely on at a time of need.

The truth is . . . I love you very much! But I am not in love. I don't know when, and if, I'll ever fall in love with a man.

For now my answer to your proposal to become your "steady girlfriend" is no. I like my freedom and my space, and I don't know if I'll ever get married. I hope I don't hurt your feelings and we can still remain friends forever.

Love ya,
Marie

In 1996, I met Anna, a beautiful Italian girl from my hometown in Italy. Anna was our Italian teacher. Our eyes crossed in the elevator and I would have loved to let her know how I felt. I saw her on the train on the way back to Australia and we never got a chance to get to know each other. We were supposed to go on a romantic Italian dinner, alone on the coast, but my wish didn't eventuate. She called me to let me know that she was sick, she was coughing, and it was raining that night. From time to time, Anna came into my mind, but I had to be realistic. She had a great job and no way in the world was she going to drop everything to come and live in Australia, and there wasn't a chance in hell that her father was going to accept a tiler, with a diploma of architecture, looking for work in Italy, to marry his daughter. Anna became my penfriend. She always wrote back to me until 1997 when I stopped writing to her. I was starting to miss her but had no money to go and see her. Three years ago, when I went back home to Italy for a week, during my trip with the soccer players, a mutual friend advised me not to go for a visit or call her because she had just gotten married. I stayed in touch with Anna until 1997.

27 July, 1996

Dear Nick,

How are you? It's a long time since I heard you. Hope you are well and busy, something good.

As far as I'm concerned, there's something new. As you can see from the address, I've moved and now I'm living on my own.

In May, they finally finished working in my flat—the problem with the floor I probably told you of—and left it covered with dust.

I was going to burst into tears when I saw my flat again in that condition. I spent the first two weeks of my holidays from school re-cleaning it, and it was awful since I'm not used to house works and I hate them! Then I started buying the first things I needed, from the obvious ones to the ones I had never thought of but which resulted in being extremely necessary.

Then I had the furniture of my bedroom moved from my parents' flat to mine. The kitchen was already finished, everything was ready, but . . . I kept staying at my parents', finding new excuses every day: today it's too hot or it's too windy or it's Saturday and I'm going out with some friends of mine.

After almost a couple of weeks, on the 16th of July, I said to myself, "Enough! Today it's the day!" I took my suitcase, I put all my summer clothes in it, and I did it. I went away from my parents' house.

It was very painful. On the first night I cried, and the next days I didn't feel much better.

The only thing which soothed me was the idea I had done the right thing.

Now I feel better even though every day I'm realizing more fully all the different aspects and consequences of this change.

Now I'm responsible of my relationship with the outside world which is no longer filtered by my parents' presence. I also feel more fully responsible of my life and I'm not completely sure of where I want to lead it to. The problem of my parents, especially of my mother who can't accept my leaving, is she feels abandoned and she can't understand why I did it to her. This makes me feel very guilty because I love her very much and because I know I'm her link with the outside world since, because of my father, they lead a very isolated life. But I think it's my life and I'm not doing anything bad. A big mess, isn't it?

But I think time will gradually solve everything (or at least, I hope so).

These are all my news; of course after all these expenses there's no money left to afford a journey to anywhere so I'm going to spend the rest of my holidays here in Bari. Never mind! There's a time for everything.

Now it's up to you. I'm waiting for news from you so please write me soon.

Take care of yourself,
Anna

February 26, 1996

Dear Nick,

How are you? Sorry for keeping you waiting so long.

But work at school is getting harder and harder. Almost every day I'm busy in the afternoon with meetings at school not to mention the usual work of correcting tests, planning tests and lessons, and all those things. Of course with the same old story. By the way, do you know that the number of poor people is increasing steadily here in Italy?

And according to statistics, families with 4 million lire a month are considered on the edge of poverty. Don't you think it is a bit exaggerated? From this point of view, when I'll be alone I'll be considered poor since my salary is about the half of the above mentioned. Not a nice thing. And to be honest, I'm already realizing that I can't afford something I could buy or do before: theatre, cinema, trips abroad, CDs books etc. These have become luxury goods since I've gone and lived on my own and it's so frustrating.

As to my flat, there was a problem with the floor. That is with the distance between tiles. I don't know the English word. Actually I've learned the Italian one recently. The material used to make it became as hard as stone. At first I was very annoyed but now I'm more relaxed. It can be solved so let's have patience.

Now what about you? Have you solved your legal problem? Hope you did. It's always so disappointing having to fight to have your rights respected, isn't it? And moreover, it would have been such a nice opportunity travelling around the world meeting new people . . .

Anyway you did your best so forget about it and move on. The wheel of fortune will turn in your favour sooner or later.

Thank you for your photocopies about our horoscopes.

It was quite interesting to read about what the characteristic of my personality should be. To tell you the truth, I'm a bit sceptical about horoscopes and personality is the result of many influences. I find it difficult to think about influence of stars too. Anyway I'm always open to new possibilities.

At the moment I'm fascinated about psychological theories even though they aren't perfect because they don't give an answer to everything. I'm really discovering a new world.

Do you believe in horoscopes, do you find them true? Tell me about this. I could change my mind about them!

Did you have a nice St. Valentine's Day?

I do hope that a nice girl has discovered your good qualities since your last letter and your life is changing. You deserve it.

As far as I'm concerned, there's nothing new. And I've even realised that this doesn't worry me. Does this mean I'm getting old?

For a couple of weeks there's a nice and kind guy, the right man after the last rude guy I met, but . . . I almost feel annoyed. My first reaction was thinking what does he want? How does he dare?

There's no room in my life for a man. Quite frightening!

Well, that's all for this time. Please write back soon. I'm looking forward to news from you.

Much love, Anna

February 13, 1997

Dear Nick,

You can't imagine how happy I was to receive your letter after so long. I must confess I had feared I wouldn't have news from you anymore.

I found your letter at my parents' so I'm wondering if you received the letter I sent you as soon as I moved here last summer. Anyway, it doesn't matter. I'll give you my address again.

I'm sorry to hear about the problems you had with Alitalia, but, since one must try to find the best in everything, you should be proud of the way you behaved, You were correct, and I think that in these occasions the more correct you are the more incorrect appears the counter's role. In other words, I think that correctness stresses incorrectness and you are right when you say that life puts us to the test. It's hard, but we have to try to be as strong as possible to pass it.

I hope things have changed and you've found a suitable job which you deserve. Anyhow you don't need to have good or great news to write to me.

I know we're so far away that it may sounds strange to consider me as a friend, since friendship needs closeness and immediate availability too, but I'm really pleased to have news from you.

As to me, I'm getting used to living on my own. It's not easy, but I think it was the right thing to do.

I've learned to do a lot of things which my parents did. I feel more responsible, thoroughly master of my life, and it's changing me a lot. It's sort of a second birth. I'm realizing I need to reorganize my life. It's not easy to explain because it's still a great mess in my mind, but I'd like to change my job, to do something I've more aptitude for; I feel a strong spiritual urgency, I have no faith, but my practice of yoga has awakened my spiritual side and now I feel on the threshold of something I can't conceive yet and I really need someone who can show me the way. As I told you, it's a big mess and I feel tired of too much thinking, but, at the same time, I think it's good. It's the real me who's coming out.

I'm not telling anyone what's happening to me because I know someone would consider me a little weird, on the contrary I've learned to know you're a sensitive person and so I know you'll understand me.

Going on with something lighter + happier, I'm an aunt! Yes, my brother who got married two years ago became a father on February 2, and since the baby is the first niece/granddaughter in my family she's immediately turned us into idiots. We have no other subject of conversation than her: Has she eaten? Did she sleep? Has she burped? We're making big plans about her future and we've suddenly discovered a children's shop where we stop for hours. It's really worrying . . . Are you an uncle too?

I don't remember how many members there are in your family.

Take care, Anna

I had another fling with Suzie, a woman who was also a few years older than me. I had a lot in common with this one, especially in the bedroom, but she didn't turn out to be as spiritual as she made out to be. She told me to get a job and I felt insulted and humiliated because I had been trying to get my life together with work and I didn't need her to remind me. This made me think that even a spiritual woman can't be trusted and will not stay with a man who no longer has a job. Could I trust a woman like this? A few days before Christmas, I took her out to dinner for the last time and after that night, I never wanted to see her again. I had always been dumped by women around Christmas and just before my birthday. It was the first time in my life that I had to settle the score with one of them. Unfortunately it had to be her.

"Om Guru Om"

Dear Nick,

Wishing you & your family a Christmas Season of peaceful moments, warm memories and very special happiness filled with love & joy that remains throughout the year ~ May 1997 bring all that you wish for & more   lots of love Suzie

In 1995, I got a job as a security guard at Crown Casino for three nights on weekends. One morning at five o'clock, I watched a scenario that I wished I hadn't seen. Six vicious security guards dragged a man outside from the bathrooms and four of them were holding him down and trying to break every bone in his body. The man was crying and repeatedly calling for help. The other two were just standing there, enjoying the brutal beating and waiting for the man to stop breathing. From the distance, I ran to stop them and remind them of the rules that had been bestowed on us when we did the course. "How about restraint within limits? Do you consider yourself men, six onto one? You are a bunch of dogs! Actually a dog would have more brains than each one of you. A dog probably wouldn't behave like this." Had I not intervened, most probably the man would have been killed then thrown into the river to make it look as if he had suicided. They all stopped and looked at me frightened, as if to say, "Who is this guy? He is not one of us." When the supervisor arrived, he shouted for me to go back to my position where, I had been placed that night. I told him to stick his job in his backside and resigned there and then. The next day the manager called me to apologise and find out exactly what had happened. After that night, I didn't want to work for that company anymore.

In 1996 came Nadia, Miss Italy in the World for Victoria. We met at a job interview for a flight attendant position for Alitalia. We didn't get the job, to go and work in Italy, and I ended up taking Alitalia and Ansett Nordstress to court for discrimination. Eventually, when the matter was heard, I won the case and was compensated. With all the unemployed looking for work in Italy, Alitalia gave the contract to recruit 240 new flight attendants to Ansett Nordstress at the arse end of the world, to work for their flights to Milan, Boston, Rome, and New York. One hundred and twenty of who-you-know had already gotten the job and were sent here to be trained. The other one hundred and twenty were Australians who couldn't speak Italian and couldn't get a European passport or visa to work in Italy. People like myself, who had completed a flight attendant course and had Qantas Advance Level 5 in Italian, could get a European passport and visa but missed out. I also found myself alone in a group interview among nine females. The panel was also all females. The questions I was asked were offensive and irrelevant for a flight attendant position, and the interview was without any doubt rigged and politically orchestrated from the start. I cursed Alitalia and Ansett for what they did to me.

FLIGHT ATTENDANTS

Flight Attendants are required for a B767 operation based in Italy.

Expected duration of the contract is for a period of Twelve (12) months with possible extensions.

Applicants must possess, or have the ability to obtain, a European Community Passport.

Preference will be given to those applicants who:-
   Speak Italian.
   Have a minimum of 12 months experience as a Flight Attendant.

Attractive salary and conditions are offered. Applicants who do not have the required 12 months experience may be accepted and provided with training.

Applications in writing, together with a recent postcard size photo should be directed to:

Flight Attendants
Nordstress (Australia) Pty. Ltd.
TNT Tower,
Tower Square
Redfern, N.S.W. 2016.

Or Fax to (02) 319 8445. (No telephone enquiries please.)

ANTI DISCRIMINATION TRIBUNAL
MELBOURNE

No. 31 of 1996

NICK ARBOREA   Complainant

-and-

NORDSTRESS (AUSTRALIA) PTY LTD   First Respondent

and

NORDSTRESS LIMITED   Second Respondent

TERMS OF SETTLEMENT

RECITALS:

A.   The Complainant has issued proceedings in the Anti Discrimination Tribunal against the
     First and Second Respondent, alleging that the First and Second Respondents have
     breached the provisions of the Equal Opportunity Act 1995 arising out of circumstances
     in which the applicant applied for a position as a Flight Attendant.

B.   The First and Second Respondent and the Applicant have agreed to compromise these
     proceedings for commercial reasons and with a denial of liability on the following terms:-

WHEREAS IT IS AGREED:

1   Nordstress (Australia) Pty Ltd agrees to pay to Mr Arborea within seven days
         from the date this Deed the sum of   in full
         and final settlement of this complaint, and all matters incidental, and inclusive of
         costs ("the settlement sum") subject to full compliance with the following terms
         and conditions:-

         (i)   on receipt of the settlement sum the Applicant consents to orders that
                 the complaint in proceedings number 31 of 1996 in the Anti
                 Discrimination Tribunal will be struck out with no orders as to costs in
                 accordance with the Minutes of Consent Orders executed and appearing
                 as Attachment A.

Nick Arborea

EXECUTED AS A DEED

SIGNED SEALED AND DELIVERED)
by NICHOLAS ARBOREA in the)
presence of:)

....
Witness

....
Rogers & Gaylard
Solicitors for the First and Second Respondents

W:\PEOPLE\JXL\#111112D.CRH

Three years later, I saw the end of Ansett and Alitalia. Today
Alitalia is on the verge of collapse and there is little chance of
being merged with another company to resurrect it. As far as I am
concerned, Alitalia and Ansett Airline got their just desserts. This
had turned out to be the greatest disappointment of my life with
work. After so much had gone wrong with work and love, Nadia's

love and great sex kept me alive for two years. She was twelve years younger than me and this relationship was doomed not to last forever, because financially I could not meet her expectations.

Dear Nick,

What can I say? You have been extremely patient with me over the past couple of months.

First of all, I want to thank you, from the bottom of my heart for all your help and support over the past couple of months. I know I have been extremely difficult and I know at times you have felt like strangling me, ha ha ha!!!

But I want you to understand that I care for you very much and maybe this relationship has taught me the communication between two lovers, friends, parents can be the hardest challenge in life.

This relationship has taught me a lot about patience and my lack of it!

As you have probably noticed, I have little patience with my parents and I find it extremely difficult to express my feelings with my parents and family.

I have been so used to not sharing any feelings, apart from being angry and mad, that you know I'm finding it very hard to change.

Anyway, I know that this change within me is not going to happen overnight, but Nick, I'm going to give it my best shot!!! That's my promise to you!

Anyway, enough about my parents Let's talk about us!

You've been a great lover and friend, you have taught me to appreciate the good things in life, you have also taught me that loving yourself comes from within. Being in touch with Mother Nature, looking after your spiritual health, is the most important thing in life.

You have also taught me that unless people go through really bad experiences in life, they never grow spiritually!

Love, Nadia

10/12/98

Dearest Nadia,

The last four months have been miserable without you. I've suffered in silence, but I never told you.

I think of you every moment of the day. I don't sleep at night anymore. I miss your company very much. Time has stood still since you left, my love.

You've taken my soul away with you and kept me under your spell all this time.

I hope this last bit was not too deep for you. I can't help being a sentimental prick. I've always being straightforward and genuine about my feelings with you. I hope that you'll respect that.

I wish to call you and see you if I could with no strings attached. If that is what you wish!

I'd be happy to see you just once in a blue moon if you'd allow me. But don't cut your bridges with me. I don't deserve a cold shoulder.

If you need to talk to someone, call me. Stop holding back. You're a stubborn goat. (You're a typical Capricorn.)

I have found you a lovesick puppy. Its name is White Wolf.

Love you very, very much,
Baci yours, Nick

In 1996, after Nadia, I met Suzanna an ex-model. I saw her a few times, and then I didn't hear from her anymore. She wrote to me a letter that you will read later on. It explains why I didn't hear from her anymore.

5th April, 1996

Dear Nick,

Long time, no see. It must be over a month and a half since we last spoke.

I apologize for my missed date with you. I have been having a very difficult time with myself.

Well, it's difficult trying to properly explain in a brief letter, and to someone who I don't know well, but I shall attempt in a few words. I have found myself subject to unreasonable and almost unmanageable levels of anxiety recently.

And for this, I may not be staying at my own address at the time being. I found it unbearable to wake up here alone and with the sort of thinking (disastrous and not hopefully at all) that I've been unable to shift from. I also found it hard to call people around me when I wake in a frightened and negative mood.

People have offered the opportunity to drop by when I feel bad or at a loose end, and then to their homes for chats and for company.

You're such a person. It's that I've been unable to reach through the anxieties of the day and nights here, enough to take up those offers of company.

I just thought it was worth letting you know that, Nick, so as to avoid you concluding whatever you may have concluded otherwise.

I have attempted two jobs since I last saw you. One I finished in a few days and the other I could not see out, due to attacks of anxiety which just overtook me.

I have spent the last week in observation at a hospital which deals with people with depression and anxiety disorders.

I have left for the Easter weekend and am due back Monday to stay for two weeks solid there.

Perhaps the doctors and psychologists, etc. at this institution will be able to shed for me some light upon what I can do on a clinical level (as opposed to all the spiritual etc. day-to-day practises which one I'm sure you know the value of, for healing and for aiding and changing a life's course).

Anyway apart from all the things meditative, healthy, and busy, that I know are potentially healing for me, I also decided that there is something physically, chemically that is wrong within my system and I gave in fully to the last test with the psych people, as it has been this difficult and frightening for me.

I found myself avoiding people, not answering doors and phones, and letting all the messages from my friends and family just pile up, and at my boyfriend's house as well.

I've felt fearful at every knock, new daily task. And I've been feeling too exhausted to do anything.

I panic when I make any decision because a million questions and possible bad and wrong outcomes occur in my mind.

Anyway I shall not go on with this type of explanation. I just felt like feeling my neighbour in on a little miscommunication.

I will see you sometime soon, Nick, no doubt when I return here in the next few weeks.

Keep well, Suzanna

Also in 1996, came Maria who wanted me to go over to show me her God, but I was too busy to be someone's toy boy again.

In 1997, I met a Japanese girl on holidays. I took her to Philip Island and showed her some of the tourist attractions in Melbourne. While I liked her, I wasn't attracted to her and didn't want to start something I didn't feel I could commit to. However, I believe she was attracted to me. She started writing to me and sending me gifts from Japan. Her letters were deep and romantically sentimental. I had never received letters like these—romantic, very feminine, and written with finesse. I could have fallen for Japanese enchantment, but I didn't allow it because I wasn't ready.

4th April, 1996

Dear Nick,

Buongiorno! Come sta?

Sorry I haven't been in touch for a long time. I hope you still remember me the much as I do.

You're always on my mind, Nick. Your music, out of Africa, and Enya's remind me of you a lot.

And I love them too. Grazie, Nick!

I've heard from Harry that you received my message late. I'm sorry that I couldn't talk to you on the phone the last night I was in Sydney. Anyway I had a lovely time in Australia.

I don't know how to thank all my friends. I'm always missing Australia.

Now I'm back to the same routine and have a kind of busy life. My new course has started on the 27th of March. So I now I have to study hard. But I cannot. I don't know why.

It's coming on to spring here. We have beautiful cherry blossoms which make me feel happy to be here in this season.

I really wish I could show you how beautiful they are one day.

Well, dear Nick, hoping everything is going well for you. See you in October or in March '97.

Aiko

4th February, 1997

Dear Nick,

What a wonderful Christmas surprise hearing from you!

Thank you so much for your cards and a beautiful picture.

You are a great artist, Nick. Nyantos my cat loves your art as much as I do. Thank you for your time sparing for us!

I was in Los Angeles in December. I have a cousin who lives there over ten years. As she's thinking to return to Japan, this will be the last chance to see her there.

She kindly took me to Grand Canyon, Las Vegas, Mexico, and some other places.

You should see Grand Canyon. It's just amazing!

Actually, it was the second time in the US. I was staying in San Diego 18 years ago.

I'm not sure whether I have changed or the US has, but I felt quite differently.

I was planning to go to Italy in March with my friend. But I have to work til September. Could you give me some information where we should visit?

First, I have to improve my Italian!

Well, Nick, I'm glad to hear that you moved. How's your new room? Better?

I'm not sure that you've received the message or not, but I called you several times in May '96. At the time, I was with TV people whom I met through my Nyantos. He was on TV in Japan and they were looking for the story in English for drama.

So I wondered if you were interested. However . . . You might have lost the chance, Nick. Anyway, if I have heard this kind of news, where shall I contact?

Well, I really hope everything is better for you now. Take good care of yourself.

Dear Nick, I'm always wishing you happiness.

Keep shining!

Much love from your white witch.

Aiko

PS This winter in Melbourne is very cold, I've heard. I hope that this package can make you warm even a little.

Happy Valentine's Day!

In 1998, just days after I had thrown away a pile of job rejections and application that didn't bring me an interview, I landed a temporary position as a security guard on a P & O cruise on Fairstar, travelling through the Polynesian islands.

I felt imprisoned working on the ship. My little cabin, which I had to share with three others, was like a prison cell. When I was off duty, I was not allowed to give information or socialise with the passengers. There were too many restrictions, working as security guard. As a social director, things may have been different. Furthermore, I had a lesbian supervisor who was always behind my back, like a vulture.

On the night when staff were allowed to celebrate.

1st December, 1998

My Nick,

Gorgeous wonder!

Came by to visit.

Not in.

Hope you're having a wonderful day.

Catch you real soon.

All smiles,
Ashley xxx

2nd December, 1998

Hi Nick!

How are you today!

Wondering where you were last night. Couldn't find you so I went alone to the late night movie—6 nights, 7 days. Great movie!

Unfortunately I was too tired to party on last night. So I went to my cabin.

Come to visit if you get a chance, or just drop me a not on when we can catch up for a drink.

Hope you enjoyed snorkelling.

Sorry I didn't come. I slept in without even realizing the time. I spent most of my day on the island relaxing, swimming, and sunbathing.

Catch ya real soon, Gorgeous!

Warm thoughts,
Ashley xx

After the two-week program ended, I got off the ship and didn't want to go back. When I went back home, I started losing weight rapidly and could not understand what was happening to me. A sunspot near the liver was spreading fast; it was melanoma cancer. I had to be operated on immediately. The week after, they called me in to give me the bad news that they had to go deeper and wider to clean it properly. It was too close to the liver. After receiving the bad news, I put the phone down and felt a peaceful feeling in the air, as if the energy around me was telling me that everything was going to be okay.

A week later, I got operated on again and I went in feeling confident that everything would go well. The miracle was confirmed when the result came back that I was all clear. Since then I have had to protect my skin when I go to the beach and get regular checks every six months.

In 1999, I met Annie, the greatest lover I've ever known. I don't know if in this lifetime I will ever have the privilege to meet another woman like her, or better.

God has his way and he has proven to me that I was wrong before. Just when I thought I had lost the best love of my life, he has always sent me someone different and better still, to compensate for the loss, to get me up on my feet again, so that I could carry on with my life. It's when we lose faith in ourselves and give up that God can't help those who can't help themselves.

If you don't give up, when love dumps you, you will find love again. I had two of the best and worst years of my life with Annie, but the sacrifice for the love I had for her was worth every tear I spilled when I missed her, when she wasn't there anymore. It's difficult for me to accept that we couldn't even remain friends and stay in touch, even once in a blue moon. We were much too close, too intimate, to allow the interference of another person to come between us. There are things in life that we will never understand as to why it had to end that way. It took me seven long years to heal and accept that all good things must come to an end. Please continue to read with these memoirs, a letter to my daughter, which will tell you the story I had with Annie.

Life for some of us can turn out to be a real motion picture. Like every good movie, it has an ending that sometimes we wished it never had.

After my story ended with Annie, between 2002 and 2004, I renovated two properties, hoping to start a renovation company that would generate my own work.

I was capable of buying cheap, refurbishing them with little money, doing all the work, and putting them back for sale on the market quickly. But once again, timing and luck were not on my side. Both properties took a long time to sell. A year went by before an agent sold both properties within a month. By then the real estate market collapsed again. I lost $20,000 on the first property and $60,000 on the second.

The banking ombudsman found that I had wasted $59,000 on interest repayments because they took so long to sell. All my hard work and efforts once again didn't pay off, and to top it off I also had a financial disaster with Westpac Bank that I am still trying to sort out.

The first property in Campbellfield was the property from hell. Only God knows what I went through and how much rubbish I had to remove from the backyard, which had served as a tip for the previous owner. There was much work to do, to restore it to a habitable condition.

How many prayers and candles I lit to get the bad spirits out and cleanse the energy in that place! When I removed the old carpet, the entire timber floor had been painted in red! From time to time, there was a goat smell in the unit. Someone in the '70s must have performed some rituals in that unit! There were two large ice-cream refrigerators full of putrefied water. I thought I was going to find skeletons in them.

I converted the empty shop at the front into a beautiful Eurasian architectural studio apartment. According to my Turkish neighbour who was related to the first couple who moved into the unit at the rear, the husband nearly killed his wife! An ambulance and the police had to be called. Fortunately, I was not there on the day to see what had happened.

The woman who moved in after they left had the real estate agent believe that she had a job as a manager of a pub in Sunshine. She turned out to be an old prostitute who had a couple of girls working for her! She turned the rear of my property into a massage parlour. I had not been aware, until the police came, looking to arrest her son, who was also secretly living there. I used to find death-threat notes on my door, because whoever was looking for him thought that my home address was his home!

The person they were searching for was living in the back unit of my shop-front apartment! I was living worried until I sold the property. For six months, they didn't pay me rent. There was nothing I could do, until the police obtained a court order to evict them.

One morning I decided to go and knock at the door to find out when I was going to get the money. I found the door smashed. When the son opened the door, I asked who had done it. He said he did. He seemed drunk or under the influence of drugs. I became furious and gave him an ultimatum: "The next time I return to collect the money, I want to find a new door or I'll put your head through it! Have I made myself clear?" Fortunately, he did not answer back in a larrikin way and I kept my cool. When I returned three days later, the door wasn't fixed, but he wasn't living there anymore.

This latest disaster with work and money took its toll! But the evil eye and curse that must have been in that property didn't end there. It continued to follow me.

In November 2004, I had a car accident that shattered my spine, and it has debilitated my nervous system.

I got out of the car feeling as if I had been crushed by a football team; the pain in the middle of my back was unbearable. I was rushed to the Alfred Hospital with a suspected fracture of the spine. I was kept in the reanimation ward overnight, feeling an electrical discharge throughout my body. Part of my legs was numb. I couldn't stand up. I could only lie down, my body straight with my face to the ceiling.

During the night, I prayed and sang all the chants I had also learned at the ashram. All I could do was meditate and hope for a miracle. The doctor who checked the X-rays saw a fracture in the spine and warned me not to move.

During the night, I felt an energy around me, as if someone was giving me a reiki healing. I felt this penetrating warmth go through the middle of my spine and over my head. Next morning, when the nurse came to wake me up to tell me that my father had come to visit me, I was able to feel my legs and stand up again. The pain in my back had vanished. The miracle overnight had occurred. Though I haven't fully recovered yet, I am grateful to God for enabling me to walk again.

Since then, I've suffered from chronic fatigue. I don't wish upon anyone the way I feel. There are days when I feel normal, but others when I can't even get out of bed.

I need to continue rehabilitation to strengthen the ligaments of my knees. In the meantime, I also have to cope with constant pain in my eyes, back, and neck. I feel like a boxer who has been knocked down too many times yet he must find the strength and the willpower to keep on fighting.

I am not ready to give up and throw in the towel. I will get out of this spiral of negativity and get back on my feet again.

Hard work, effort, talent, and know-how don't always pay off for everybody—believe me. I have been a perfect example of that. They say, "Work as if you don't need money." I was ambitious, worked hard, loved women with passion, but luck and timing haven't been on my side yet. I never put money before love. Money without love is a worthless life. "Dance like there is nobody watching." I danced like no other and could not care less who was watching. Being bold and confident doesn't necessarily get you to places in life.

"Love as you've never been hurt." I've never stopped loving, even when love did hurt. They say that behind every successful man, there is a beautiful woman. I have enjoyed some of the most beautiful women in the world, which some men may never have. I haven't known one woman who will stay with a man without money and live on love alone. If I was financially wealthy, there was no guarantee that money would buy me their love.

And if I went to Hollywood, what would I do that I haven't already done? I would give half of my annual revenue to charity, without asking for a deduction. I learned that the best things in life don't last forever; plans and expectations can bring disappointments because nothing is guaranteed.

The most precious things are free, and they can't be bought.

When I walk down the river alone, I look at the water, the beauty of Mother Nature that surrounds me, and I take three deep breaths. I feel alive.

When I watch the sun go down, late in the afternoon on a bright clear day, I am in peace. In that moment, I feel that the creator we call God is with me and when I think of those who are less fortunate than me, I am grateful to life, because with all the blows I had to endure, there have been some miracles along the way.

CHAPTER 2
A Letter to My Daughter

My Dearest Angel,

When you were born, there was no treasure more valuable than you and your mother that a man could ever find in life. You were eight years old when I wrote this letter, which I am sending to you as you are now a woman and old enough to understand, so that you can make up your own mind about this story I have had with your mum eighteen years ago.

You might not care to hear what I'm about to say, but you have the right to find out what happened during the first two years of your life. Your mum had to cut you out of my life before you could talk and understand, because you were beginning to call Joe "Nick" when he got home from work. Whenever you heard your mum talking to me on the phone, you'd crawl up her legs and you would not stop crying unless she put you on the phone.

You were just happy to hear my voice and say those few words you had already learned: "Heei, Nick," "Yep," and "Bayii!" Only then would you shut up!

Please continue to read this letter and allow me to explain who I am and why I wasn't allowed to be in your life. Only God knows how desperate I was and how many tears I've spilled because your mum didn't want to see me anymore after she met Tom Edison. She made that choice, and I had to respect her wish. As much as it hurt me to be kept away from you, I couldn't understand and accept why I wasn't even allowed to remain a friend at a distance! What wouldn't I have done just to be able to see you once in a blue moon, or at least at Christmas, your birthday, and Easter? I had to keep away, otherwise one of the three men in your mother's life could have been seriously hurt over a woman, and one of them could have ended up in jail.

I met Natalie and her sisters Cara and Isa at the Tycoon Night Club in July 1999. They were regulars there. They went to this venue every Thursday and Saturday night. They were the centre of the attraction, the heart and soul of dance and its transgressive R & B fashion. The manager always had a bottle of Champagne and a table reserved for the girls. I was treated like a VIP by the bouncers and the girl at the door.

Since the day I met your mum until the last time we danced together, I never had to pay for a ticket to get in. Your mum and her sisters all gave me the same storyline that they were all married with a husband and children at home, while they danced the night away until three in the morning! In a pick-up place like that, who would believe them? I took it as an excuse that they used to keep men away. Soon though, I found out that Cara and Isa were both having affairs—Cara was with a Greek man who was divorced, a teacher who was almost fifteen years older than her, and Isa had a different bloke around her every week. I only met Cara's husband once. He dropped in one night to see if the girls were behaving. When he arrived, Peter, Cara's man on the side, finished dancing with her, said goodbye, and left for the night.

I had already seen your mum four times before we became close and intimate. She told me that she was separated and waiting for her divorce to be finalized. I didn't know what to make of her story. I had made a vow to myself years ago to keep away from any woman who told me she was divorced or separated. The Devil always knows our weakness, and this time he made me an offer too good to pass. Your mum offered me the apple, like Eve to Adam. I fell for it and took the bite.

It happened two weeks before my thirty-ninth birthday, at 2.30 a.m. at the rear of the Glen Waverley freeway after we dropped off your Aunt Isa. She pulled over and asked me to get into her car, because my two-seater Porsche wouldn't have been appropriate for sex. I realized she didn't want to go just for a coffee. She was giving me the hint that she was after something more.

When she pulled over on the side of the road, she began to complain about her husband Joe, saying how he had neglected her, that he had made no attempt to kiss and make up to get back together since they had split up. She said "You men are all the same. Nobody wants me. You are just like the rest of them. That's why I left Joe." I replied, "Darling, you are stunning! There is nothing wrong with you. It's just that when men hear that you're separated, they don't know what to make of your story. How do I know if you're telling me the truth? As much as I trust you, you could still be living with him. This is why, after all this time, I still haven't made a pass at you."

She kissed me and thanked me for helping her see common sense and explaining why men didn't want to go near her. She then moved from the driver's seat to on top of me.

She had a miniskirt that looked like a black nightie, with stiletto shoes and the body of a goddess. She was gorgeous.

We were both aroused. Before we had sexual intercourse, I recall that she warned me to be careful, to make sure I put the condom on properly as she wasn't on the pill and it was the dangerous time of the month. That night was the first time that your mother and I made love.

The unexpected happened—the condom broke and before I realized what had happened, it was too late. I quickly reached for the tissues to cover up the mess. She turned around and immediately asked, "You didn't come in me, did you?." I said, "No." I was too embarrassed to admit it. I truly believe that you were conceived at that moment, that very night.

The same night she told me that she couldn't see me for a few weeks, because she had family commitments and parties to attend to. I knew this was too good to be true: she fucked me and now she doesn't want to see me anymore. I thought that, after that night, I would never see her again.

To my surprise, the phone rang again five weeks later. She invited me to meet up with her at Tycoon again. That night when I looked into her eyes, after all that time, I said, "Annie, you are pregnant." She replied, "My God, how did you guess?" Talking about telepathy! We must be connected.

From that night onward, she called me every day. There were times that she'd ring me up to three times a day. I thought that her behaviour was controlling, almost obsessive, but I must admit I enjoyed all the attention, love, affection, and great sex, which I had never received from other girlfriends before your mum.

I will never forget that night—it was raining heavily. I was feeling tired and had no energy to go out. I was about to go to sleep. As soon as she called me, I felt recharged—I had an adrenalin rush to see her.

The rain and the wind stopped by the time I got to the beach; the clouds in the sky cleared the beautiful white full moon and the stars came out to shine on us; and the sea calmed down. It seemed as if the gods were happy to see us together.

I held her hand and said, "Look at the sky and see if we can catch a fallen star. As soon as you see it, make a wish." We both saw one fall. When I asked her what she wished for, I discovered that she made the same wish that I had made for her. It was to have the most beautiful little girl, who would look like her or one of her sisters. You turned out to be stunning, as if I had imagined you would be, with the Brigitte Bardot lips like your mother and Aunt Cara. That night, we caught three falling stars. I also wished our love to last for eternity, and financial success so that I could provide for her if she left Joe. I used to buy her a handful of the biggest cherries that I could find; I used to pick them one by one. I couldn't buy her favourite pink tulips for her, because she couldn't take them home. Joe would have questioned her.

I nicknamed her Cherry Lips. I didn't just love your mother, I adored her more than anything in life.

For two years and two months, she called me every second night to meet up at our regular spot at Brighton Beach or in Seaford, which was our meeting point halfway for both of us. During the nine months of her pregnancy, I did not sleep to protect her and the child that was growing in her tummy to make sure that they both got home safe when we left the beach at three in the morning. How many times I used to say to her it was time to go home. And she would say, "I don't want to go!" I fed you with love and affection when your mother and I were happy under the stars and the moon. I took the risk to stand by her when she needed me to be there for her during the difficult period of her pregnancy. I fathered you, Angel, until you were two years old, until your mum cut me out of your life.

She always complained that her husband neglected her sexually, was cold and careless, and refused to hear her warning bells to make changes in order to save their relationship. I remember her telling me that he once went for a business meeting at the Rosebud Country Club, where he boasted to his brothers-in-law that he had the whole executive suite to himself and could not be bothered driving back home that night, knowing he had a pregnant woman who could have the baby at anytime.

I often wondered if this man really cared for Natalie or had any concerns for what she got up to. They must have had some kind of marital arrangement, or he must have trusted his wife so much, or turned a blind eye. He probably wasn't sure whether the child about to be born was his or not. One night he would stay home with the boys and the next she would stay home so he could go out with his mates. According to your mum, he must have had another woman on the side, because he had lost his loving feeling and appetite for her.

After you were born, whenever we went away for the weekend, we always took you along with us in the basket. Our trips included going to my parents' beach house in Rye and renting a cottage in Dandenong and Philip Island. I'd often meet up with her on a Friday night, when she went shopping at Fountain Gate Shopping Centre. Her husband would stay home with the boys and she always felt safe to meet and catch up for a coffee if she wasn't coming into the city to go dancing.

I hated her for leaving you at home with Joe while she'd be dancing away with me and her sisters until three in the morning. Natalie never gave me an explanation as to why she was leaving me, why she decided to suddenly cut me out of her life. She didn't even allow me to remain a friend. I believe that when she met the third male, Paul Ericson, a shoe salesman who made her believe he was the manager of that shoe shop, she had to cut one out of her life. It had to be me because financially I could not look after her and I never suggested to her that she should leave her husband. I couldn't take her away from Joe.

She could never compare me to her husband. What would she say to her parents? That she was leaving her husband, an account manager of a software company, for a struggling tiler who wanted to become a builder?

One night at Tycoon, she went off to dance with a shady character. From time to time, she always danced with different men who were introduced to the group by her sisters. This outsider was one that didn't feel safe. I had a terrible gut feeling about him and my intuition had never failed me. I looked at her as if to say, "What are you doing?" She grinned as if to say, "Are you jealous?" and then went on the floor with him.

I thought that she was going to have just a dance or two and come back to the table, like she usually did. This time she got carried away and continued to dance with him—even to our favourite song. When she returned to the table, she asked me to dance. I said, "You've got to be joking." I picked up my jacket, looked at him, and left. Since that night, our relationship was never the same. She rang me three days later, begging me to pick up the phone. I would hear her message, give her two rings, and put the phone down.

I had promised her that if she ever played games with me, for three months she would never hear my voice. I would let her know that I got the call but wouldn't speak to her until I felt good and ready to forgive her. I told her that I would do this so that she had the time to assess her life and make up her mind with what she wanted. I had to do it. I had to put my foot down to see if she really loved me.

When she needed me desperately, she would ring me at anytime of the night. She'd drive all the way to my parents' place to leave me a note behind the door, to let me know how much she was missing me. This time the phone stopped ringing. Two weeks before we split up, she apologized and wrote a card to me with a bear gripped to a trunk, apologizing for being such a bitch for playing games. She had a mania to ring me and invent a new story every day.

She had an imagination! She could brush up a novel a day if she set her mind to write down what she created in her head. One day, it was about the postman making compliments, another about the real estate agent who dropped in to evaluate the property, and then there was the forty-five-year-old Indian cousin on her mum's side who dropped in at lunchtime and at one time tried to rape her when your father was overseas for a business trip. It got to the point where I didn't know whether she did it to stir me, to see if she could make me jealous or to tease me to see how I would react, or even if there were other lovers dropping in on the side. She asked me to forgive her, said she would never do it again, and that I was the best thing that had ever happened to her life.

That night, I could not believe what the Devil had gotten into her to leave me, her lover on the side, and to throw everything away which we had shaped for more than two years, to try out another man!

After all I did for her, to give her all the love, attention, and sex she could not get from Joe, according to her. I kept my word and then when I finally decided to call her a month later, she told me that she had started seeing Paul. She didn't waste any time to move on, as she would say. Never in my wildest dream did I think she would be like that.

I told her that before she jumped the gun, I wanted both of us to take a DNA test to determine if you were my daughter. At first she agreed, then she changed her mind, then she got Tom to interfere and tell me what to do. I felt hurt and humiliated and never imagined that she would allow another person to come between us. He began to make threats to prove to her that he could protect her and stop me from asking her about the DNA.

But I could not give up on finding out if you were my daughter or not. I had to know. I missed you as much as I missed your mum in a different way. I even ended up seeing a female family counsellor, hoping that I could get her to make your mum speak to me and referee between us, but she refused the conciliation meeting, forcing me no other alternative but to take the matter to court to request the DNA. I waited two years. In the meantime, there were threats and restraining orders thrown to both sides. I wanted the DNA to be able to get a court order to visit you when it would be convenient for your mum.

DNA was wrong! When I got the test, I only had three codes relating to you out of seven. Accordingly to the genetic law, for a man to be considered the true father, he has to have four or five codes. I missed out by one. Whatever happened at the time, I was not convinced that I found out the truth. In my view, someone purposely tampered with the test or made an error when reading the finding.

My conspiracy theory is that your grandfather had friends in high places who could have done him a favour at the forensic department, to give me one code less, to exclude me out of your mum's life, or that the French analyst decided to write one code not matching up to scratch to favour your mum because she felt sorry for her circumstances. I was not convinced that the result of the DNA test was the truth.

Regardless of how the result turned out, I feel that you have been, and always will be, my daughter, in my heart. No one can take that away from me! After the experience I've had, next to your mum, watching you grow, until you were two years old, no one can deny that you wouldn't feel like a daughter to me. I decided then that there wasn't going to be another child for me with another woman. I also decided that eventually I would live with someone but never get married.

Should you ever need me, know that you'll always have another father who you can turn to, who you can count on for anything. I will always be there for you.

Love from Nick, your Tati Dadaha.

30 October, 2007

Dear Nicola,

After seeing you on Tuesday night, I left you and made my way home with the deepest sadness and emptiness.

And if you can allow 10 minutes of yourself to be a friend, to allow me to write and express these few words.

In the few hours that we were alone, I watched you. Allowing yourself going from one emotion to the next. I watched you cry, smile, talk, be sad, be just who you are. You don't know how much that meant to me.

I am so blocked up inside that I cannot understand how to feel and how to allow it. I find myself so detached to everything around me. And detached from my feelings. You have no idea how painful this is. I feel as though I do not exist. You have no idea how much it meant to me to be in your company. That was far more important to me than the sexual experience. I learned so much in those few hours. I may be

developed physically, but you are my teacher emotionally. Although I am your friend, I so need a friend.

See you soon,
Robyn

2 November, 2007

Nikky,

Baby, please let's start over with the friendship. I was totally out of line.

I was disappointed with the universe, because it failed to give me exactly what I needed and the frustration was just eating at me. But reflecting on it, I see that this is where I need to be and need to experience. So I'm letting go from the expectation.

I sincerely appreciate your friendship, and emotionally you are my guide. I am grateful that I have you at this point in my life. Above all, I enjoy your sexual company immensely and the warmth. Some women never get to experience this.

I will be a friend to you, with no expectations. I can see how much you're going through and hurting inside over your loss. Yet you are willing to offer the warmth. This is appreciated.

With the deepest desire, hope to see you.

Robyn

3 November, 2007

I will be asking God himself to why some women are gifted with profound beauty, externally and internally. Yet some women are not. How is this? How does he make a choice like this?

I'm really angry with him. I demand an answer, especially knowing how much I suffered in one of my past lives cause of the lack of beauty. Anyhow I leave this scenario at this.

Ciao, baby.

Robyn

CHAPTER 3
Poems of Love

To Nick, Thinking of you, with love. Virginia Elisabeth.

My Twin Soul Mate

To Nick,

I am grateful for all that you are

For all that you've done for me.

You are a very special person, one of a kind, someone whom anyone would be privileged to meet.

You are a treasure; don't let anybody tell you otherwise.

You've been the most lovable, caring, generous, and pleasing lover I've ever known.

Your love has spoiled me.

I love making love to you. It feels so good, so right.

You are a beautiful lover.

This kind of chemistry only happens once in a lifetime, and I know that I can never love anyone else the way I've loved you.

I've always known what I wanted from love, and now that I have found all that I want in you, I don't want anybody else.

It's so nice to have found someone who understands me, someone who I don't always have to explain myself to, who accepts me for who I am.

Doing nothing with you makes me happy just to be with you.

It's very rare to find one's twin. I am so fortunate to have found you.

If time should ever keep us apart, I will hold you on the unforgettable memories.

Love, I hate it when we argue.

I must stop playing games, I promise.

I've been a real bitch this week, you know what I mean. I make a big thing out of nothing.

You're surely the best thing that's ever happened to me. Hang in there, forgive me,

Love you forever,
Natalie

Why You Were So Special

By Nicholas Arborea

My Dearest Natalie,

You were my kick-start to every morning, the light of a dark day. You gave me reason to live.

You were everything I've ever dreamed to find, all that I've ever wanted from life in a woman.

Now that you're gone, nothing pleases me anymore.

There is nothing out there that can make me happy; can't get no satisfaction.

You were a strong shoulder of moral support for me, a tower of strength.

Only God knows if I'll ever find it again.

Your love had the magic to make things happen, believe it. Anything would have been possible with you by my side. Your beauty, femininity, sensuality, and eroticism have kept me under your spell. How can I forget you, even after all this time?

You made me feel wanted, loved. No woman before you had given me so much care and attention.

You were always there for me. This is why I still miss you. Your memories of the good times we've shared are a precious gift of life, and no one can take that away from me. These will always prevail and overcome every evil and jealousy that came between us to tear us apart.

That's why I have forgiven you and I hope that you can forgive me. I never blamed you for what happened to us, because I was just as stubborn and proud as you to talk things over.

A long time has passed and years will continue to pass by, but time will never forget Annie. She'll always have a place in my heart.

We have a telepathic connection that will never be broken, I will always feel your vibes in the air no matter how distant (separate) we are.

Other men may have taken your body, but not your heart and soul. You might deny that; deep down I know that you are not happy. In spirit you are with me wherever I go, there will always be a place, a song, a French movie that will remind me of you.

This is why you are so special to me, and I will always be there for you should you need to turn to me.

I've loved you, still love you, and forever will.

From the other half of you,

Should time keep us apart, I will hold you in my unforgettable memories Nick, you're the greatest lover I've ever known, love you for eternity. Your amore, Anni Marie.

When I found You, I Was the Richest Man in the World

By Nicholas Arborea

My Dearest Annie,

They say that in life, when you find a real friend that you can count on, you've found a real treasure.

You were the most precious gem that I've ever found.

Then someone came along one day and stole that treasure from me. Since then, not only have I lost the dearest friend I had, I also lost my happiness and all the pleasure and joy that you brought to my life. Even after all this time, I'd like to thank you for having been the best two years of my life.

I hope that you have forgiven me for how it ended between us two, as I have forgiven you. There was no winner, and the score between us was not a draw. We both lost.

If you can forgive and forget, then we can save the friendship. It's never too late to be friends again.

Love from a friend who will always be there for you, despite what happened,

No red wine, no party! To Nick with love. Marianne Kitten.

The Meaning of Love

By Nicholas Arborea

Love is to give to another person without expecting anything from them in return.

Love is total dedication to one person whom you love.

There is no temptation for another. You see no other person better than him or her. You don't see grass greener on the other side.

Love is not attachment or obsessive behaviour as if you can't live without them.

Love is free, unconditional, because you should feel safe with that person.

Never worship anybody before God. When you do, you lose yourself. He or she will be taken away from your own insecurity, fear, and doubt.

This is why love can be great pleasure and pain. No one knows the real meaning of love unless they have suffered for it.

Look at what Jesus had to suffer for our love, for the sake of humanity, to save our souls.

When love leaves you, and you know within your heart to have done your best to please them, set them free. Be in peace with yourself; don't leave your soul behind with them.

No human being is worth more than you.

If they come back, they were yours; if they don't, they weren't meant to be.

So be glad to have loved and known love than not to have loved at all.

Nick, you are like a light that shines in the darkness of the rest of the world. Much love, Diana.

Are You a Season, a Reason or a Lifetime?

By Nicholas Arborea

When people come for a season, they are sent to us to fulfil a wish that we've put out to the universe. They bring us an experience we need to share and learn in order to grow.

They may teach us something you have never done before. These are our teachers or our students. They bring us a lot of pleasure and joy. That seems like real love, but it's only for a season.

When they come for a reason, they come at a time of need, to assist us through a difficult period. They provide us guidance, support, to aid us emotionally, physically, and spiritually. They are godsends, which is why we get attached.

Then, without any reason or wrongdoing by you, when you least expect it, at an inconvenient time, they will do or say something to end the relationship.

Sometimes they walk away without an explanation. At other times, they force us to take a stand. What we must understand and accept is that their work is done, they had to go, and we must move on. Often these people are too good to be forever. That's why they are not meant to be.

A lifetime partner accepts you for what you are. Through the good and bad, they never leave you no matter what you do. They will always love you. That's why they say, "Love is blind."

When you figure out which one it is, you will know what love is.

You're always on my mind Nick, your music Out of Africa and
Enya's remind me of you. Lots of love from your Aiko.

Missing You

By Nicholas Arborea

If only the stars, the moon that once shone the night for us, could tell you how much I've missed you. What wouldn't I do just to hear your voice again and to be able to hold you in my arms like I used to.

You felt my vibes, heard my calling, but you didn't come back. Sometimes in life it's easier to let go of a loved one who has passed away, knowing that they are gone and not coming back, than to know that they are alive but can't be with you. Where there was love, you can forgive. When there is care, you can help.

If you reach out, it's never too late to make a fresh start and not repeat the same mistakes.

Always in my heart and mind, with all my love,

Nick, I thought you had forgotten me. Love Danii

To Love

By Nicholas Arborea

You that you are as warm as the sun, supreme master of life.
You come with the beauty and passion of Venus, the sweetness
and ecstasy of spring.
You fascinate me with the magic of your mystery and keep me
under your spell.
You've been the greatest joy and pain of my life.

You cared for me and shared so much, then you always leave
me lonely in the end.
Each time you've come back into my life over the centuries,
I tried so hard to get to know you and understand your lessons.
I have never been able to conquer you and keep with me forever.
I have come so close yet so far from being all that you are.
You are like a butterfly that keeps on flitting away.
I just wish that someday you come to stay,
So that I can merge in you and become all one for eternity.
Peace, joy, harmony forever with all my heart and soul.

Thank you for teaching me how to appreciate Mother Nature and keep the spiritual side of me in balance with my physical, my confidence and beauty has bloomed since I've been with you. Thank you, Nick. With gratitude and love, Angela.

Unforgettable

By Nicholas Arborea

Here's the thing about me.

I could always see the future, but I lived for the present.
I learned that nothing in life is guaranteed to last forever.
I see flashes of my past and all the things that let me down,
memories I don't want to remember ever again.

I see only one woman who made me really happy and I miss her.
Today I wish I could tell her how much I still love her.
Tomorrow my love for her will never die.
I just wanted her to know how I wish so much to have her back.

Bodyguard steps in to save snappers from beating

BODYGUARDS would not normally offer protection for the paparazzi.

But photographers chasing **Katie Holmes** oddly found themselves being rescued from a fight by the Hollywood actress's bodyguard in Carlton last Friday.

A witness to the stoush said Holmes ducked into San Churro chocolate shop on Lygon St while on a break filming horror flick *Don't Be Afraid of the Dark*.

Six paparazzi then tried to photograph her through the shop's front window.

"Then this table of tough guys got up and began yelling at the photographers to leave the lady alone," the witness, who did not wished to be named, said.

He said an argument then started between the two groups.

"These guys began pushing and threatening the photographers and it started to get pretty scary," he said.

"All of a sudden her bodyguard, who looked like a big version of **Tom Sellick**, came out of the shop and broke up the fight.

"He definitely saved the paparazzi from being bashed."

The next day, Holmes took a break from filming to spend some quality family time with husband **Tom Cruise** and daughter **Suri** at the Royal Botanic Gardens.

Passers-by saw the pair cuddling as Suri slept in Holmes' arms by the lake near Government House.

When I Almost Bashed the Paparazzi and Tom Cruise's Bodyguard

Katie Holmes's spineless bodyguard did nothing to protect her privacy and snappers from their assault on her.

He stood by the door frightened as a verbal argument broke between one man and four of the six paparazzi who came running from every direction with their binocular cameras that looked like baseball bats, forcing the celebrity to run into the chocolate shop.

To set the record straight, the bystander went to her rescue after she had walked in the shop. He found himself alone, surrounded by six paparazzi who were pushing him to get out of their way, claiming to be doing their job. The man shouted, "There is a limit to how you do your job. Get out of my sight. Stand back. You've been warned! Leave her alone. Let her have a coffee in peace, bloody idiots. Fuck off."

There was no fight for her security guard to intervene and try to break up. There was no table of tough Carlton guys yelling, or pushing or verbal threats made by more than just one man. The witness does not wish to be named because he is a coward who is trying to make a name for his mate.

Two acquaintances of the man heard him yell, so they ran from the nearby café Stuzzichino to see what was happening. Tom Cruise's wife's bodyguard was a show pony who walked in front of her like a shadow. He appeared to be more like a catwalk model than a gorilla. He apparently knew one of the six paparazzi because he called him by his name—from the doorway he shouted, "Jason, enough now!" This was all he did to save them from a probably well-deserved beating. If anything, he would have been in it with them if a fight broke out. In my view, he was their informer, telling them of every move where the Cruise family would be next.

I suggest that if Mr. Cruise is serious about protecting his wife and children, he should keep an eye on whom he employs for their protection. I was a casual security guard to celebrities who happened to pass by and reacted on natural instinct to restrain the vultures (paparazzi) who have no consideration for what they do. After what happened to Princess Diana, I would not have allowed anybody to come so close to Katie and Suri, if I was working for their protection.

Nicholas Arborea

Artist and former security guard to the stars who argued with four of the six photographers, for the welfare of the Cruise family.

CHAPTER 4
Revelation of a Mystery

Believe It or Not!

They say that the spirit of Casanova never really died, that it's out there somewhere. A seventeenth-century alchemist taught him the secret of everlasting life.

When I heard about it on a TV show called *Voyager* on the Italian channel of Optus Pay TV, I said he must have been reincarnated in his next life into Don Juan (Don Giovanni) and then Rudolph Valentino, the great lover of women at the turn of the twentieth century.

I hope now Nick Arborea can finally give Casanova's soul a rest once and for all with the closure of this book. Check www.voyager.rai. it for the Italian TV show on unresolved mysteries, which aired on RAI International Sky Channel on 18 May, 2009.

The discovery I made was on 16 July, 2009, two months later.

When Giacomo Casanova died in 1798, he didn't finish his book but managed to complete a theatrical play for Mozart called *Don Giovanni (Don Juan)*. Casanova had written about his next life before he died. He even knew the exact name of the person who his spirit would have possessed: Don Giovanni.

This type of revelation can only be made by a guru, a great spiritual master, or a mystic. Casanova must have been a medium.

Without any doubt, the magnetism of his eyes hypnotised, spellbound his women, and to seduce them he knew exactly what to say and what to do at the right time. When I was trying to complete this book, I felt that there was still something missing that I had not yet included but needed to be revealed.

I could not also make up my mind on the title, so I decided to consult a renowned medium to read it and give it a title.

She called it *The Story of My Life,* and then she changed her mind and called it *My Love Life.* She would be a witness and swear that she never had read the book on the life of Casanova. it's bizarre how initially she gave me the same title for my book, which I eventually ended up calling *The Mystery of My Life.*

So, how on earth did I know that Casanova's spirit lived on in Don Juan (Don Giovanni) and then Rudolf Valentino? I hadn't even read Casanova's book before 16 July, 2009, and I made the prediction two months before on 18 May, 2009.

Coincidence? No! Nothing in life happens by chance. It's all meant to be.

Our subconscious can bring up associations from our past when we least expect it, and it all happened also at a time of a month of this year in June, when the planets Chiron, Neptune, and Jupiter had aligned for that reason, to bring up debris of the past to surface.

What makes my comparison credible? I also discovered, as I read Casanova's book *The Story of My Life,* that Casanova and I had more than one thing in common. His women were also Venetian (from the Veneto area in Italy), Greek, and French, and the majority of the women I have known are also from these three countries. I have also written songs and ideas for new movies, like Casanova.

Please continue to read. The best is yet to unfold.

A few months ago, at the Victorian Spiritual Union where I go every Sunday, I met a man called Tim who looked like Jesus: a peaceful character like the one we've seen in movies, photos, and church paintings.

He told me that he knew exactly where to find me and that he had something very important to tell me about my life. Before he explained what the matter was about, to make me believe in him, he wanted to give me a demonstration. When he went outside, he raised his hand like Adolf Hitler toward a street lamp that was turned off, and, whatever he did with the power of his mind, he turned it on.

He told me that a small man, almost a midget, knew secrets that gave him the power to control anyone at his will, but went the wrong way about it. I could not believe my eyes.

I had seen a trick like that on TV performed by David Copperfield, but never before that night live. He told me that he had come to redeem me. According to him, Casanova's spirit had possessed me in his last reincarnation in 1961. Because after Don Juan, he didn't get to fulfil his existence when he reincarnated in Rudolf Valentino. Valentino's life was cut short when the Mafia had him killed in the hospital. He didn't die from an appendix operation—he was poisoned for jealousy. Men of all walks of life envied him. He had enemies; women of powerful men betrayed their husbands to have affairs with Valentino. In those days, divorce was not an option. It was considered a scandal—some men believed that it was better to get rid of the lover of their wife than to divorce. He was the star of the cinema in the early movies and the first *sexiest man of Hollywood*. According to Tim, this is why in this life, since I was a child, I longed to go to Hollywood: to complete the life for Valentino where he left it. I was living two lives in one body.

He told me that he was going to perform an American-Indian shaman ritual to free my soul from the repetitive cycle. This was going to be the last time that Casanova's life and soul would be tormented and pursued by the same women. I joked with him and asked if I was going to lose my appetite for women. He said, "No."

"Your eyes will look but no longer suffer for the desire that has kept you bound for centuries to all the same women you've bumped into again and again. When the right one comes next time, you'll be able to recognise her. Because she will come to you. This time, she will be true love," he said.

I also told him that it was said in the Bible that he would be back, at the turn of the new millennium. I said, "This time you are not here to be put on the cross, are you?" He said, "No."

He told me that he was in battle already, and he had a lot of work to do in silence to help humanity. He knew beforehand that Obama would win the election, and he gave me the winning horse of the Melbourne Cup. To play it safe, I put only ten dollars on it and won $350. If only I had listened to him, I may have made a fortune. I didn't trust it because last year I had lost fifty dollars.

TJ (Tim Jesus) told me that President Obama's grandmother passed away hours before his election as a sacrifice to humanity. Obama's mother died in Hawii for selfless service to others. They both triumphed from spirit to finally seeing blacks and whites starting to unite as one.

I told TJ that I had already died in this life and resurrected—after Annie left me, my last relationship that ended in 2002. And since then, I haven't looked like that Nick nor behaved like him, when Casanova lived in me.

He said that he knew about it, which is why he came up to find me to complete the ritual—so that I could start living a new life.

Tim had come to the Victorian Spiritual Union by tram. After we had a coffee in South Melbourne, I gave him a lift back home. I dropped him off somewhere in Richmond. He didn't want me or anybody to know where he lived.

He left America because he had to come back to where time had begun. It had something to do with the aborigines and the upcoming change to the world that will commence from 2012 onward.

As I drove him back that night, I told him how I died at the end of 2003. My whole family was in Italy. It turned out that they all had gone except me.

It was the first time that I had found myself totally alone in Australia, with all my family and relations in Italy. That night at 9.30, as I was watching a Bollywood movie and thinking of my ex, time stopped and I blacked out. I was reawakened by a phone call thirty-five hours later. When I woke up, I realised it was daylight. The clock on the wall showed 2.30 p.m. The time on my wristwatch had stopped at 9.30.

I felt as if someone had knocked me at the back of my head. I asked my friend Tony what day it was, and he said Thursday. I replayed where I had been all this time. Last time I remembered, I was watching a movie and it was Tuesday night at 9.30 p.m.

I dropped Tim off. He took my number and said that he would keep in touch. Since that night, I have never seen him again.

CHAPTER 5
The Mask of Pan

Who is Pan, and what has the Mask of Pan got to do with Casanova and myself? Pan was the primal male incarnate spirit descended among us in human form, and the most powerful spirit that could please women like no other man in the bedroom. He came before Casanova or any other great lover who has come from his bloodline. Pan in the Greek-Roman mythology was the great earthly deity of love, passion, and Mother Nature's wilderness, worshipped by the pagan and the Arthurians.

He was born a freak: half man, half animal with the little horns of a goat and a penis hung like a horse. Pan was a shepherd abandoned by his parents as a child and left in the forest alone to survive on his own. It is said in the legend that when Pan blew his cane flute, all the witches and virgins ran to him by the riverbanks.

There was no jealousy among them. They all shared him and took him in turn to have sex with him. He had plenty of lust to please all of them. Rose, a friend of mine, certainly experienced the spirit of Pan in me the night after she met me.

That night, at that very same time, I was writing about Pan to complete this book, Rose was being possessed by the spirit entity and experiencing the most powerful sexual experience that any woman could have. When I saw her again a few days after, she was a bit embarrassed to explain what had happened to her the night after she met me, because it was something she couldn't speak about to anyone, otherwise they'd think she was going loony.

She told me that during her sleep she was awakened by a weight on her chest. She saw a twirling, white cloud in front of her as she opened her eyes. She heard a strong male voice telling her to let go and enjoy. "From now on, take it as it comes. Don't resist it."

She felt a penetrating thrust of pain and pleasure in her vagina, and it opened up all her chakras. The depth and width of her vagina had been stretched to the maximum like never before. The ghost that had possessed her was giving her an endless, mind-blowing orgasm that went on and on and on, nonstop.

The voice continued to say, "Enjoy, enjoy. This is what it will be like from now on." She was left fused by the pleasure of the ecstasy of her orgasms. The next morning she felt exhausted and enchanted in the most blissful, peaceful, harmonious state.

When I saw Rose again a few days later, I had no intention to end up sleeping with her. I was finally in peace with myself and I wasn't ready to start another relationship with any woman yet. I had made it clear to Rose that our relationship would go no further than just friends. She made me a coffee, in front of me. I had my eyes on what she was doing in the kitchen—I even put in the sugar. But after I drank it, I felt dizzy, as if the coffee had been spiked. Something strange was happening to me. I couldn't get up from the sofa. I was not in any condition to drive home. Rose offered me to sleep over.

By the early hours of the morning, unwillingly we ended up having sex. I got up unusually aroused, horny like never before. It was up until I finished with her that we both realised that something mysterious had come between us. Not only was I able to please her like no other man had ever done before me, but when she looked down on me, she noticed that the size of my penis had become almost twice the length and wider than what I usually am. It took three days before it returned to my usual size.

Pan wanted to let me know that he was still around us that night and to remind me that he came before Casanova, Don Juan, Rudolf Valentino, and me.

When Rose met with her friends a few days later, they all noticed a change in Rose's face. In their eyes, it seemed that she had been physically rejuvenated. There was a glow in her aura that they had never seen before.

Her friend Bev, who is a spiritualist, said that when I was writing about Pan I had evoked his spirit and, as she thought of me at the same time, she attracted Pan's spirit to go to her telepathically.

I didn't know why I made a papier-mâché head of a horned man in high school. I was just a teenager. I had no idea what it meant or the spirit I was reawakening, or the puzzle I ended up discovering years later. I won first prize, and my friends, out of sheer jealousy, threw it out of the truck on the way back from the exhibition. Sometime later, I moulded one out of clay, and again I won the first prize for clay works.

The Egyptian art teacher wanted to take it away with him at Box Hill Tech., I convinced him to give it back to me as a memory of high school days, and eventually my mum put it away in a glory box. For years, it didn't come out from where she had hidden it.

My kid brother had also dreamed that I was fighting a man with horns. I wrote about it in my first article for my high school magazine in 1976. It was years later I discovered the meaning of that dream and the missing piece to the puzzle.

That horned mask with a grinning smile had drawn numerous attractive women into my life for sex, but none of them fell in love or came back to me after we'd split up. I had lost count of the women I had dated to try to find true love—I was exhausted.

I could never get over it or understand how some junkies, drug dealers, or characters that beat up their women ended up with beautiful women who have remained attached to them, and I still can't find one from all the women I have known who will stay with me. I couldn't understand why timing and luck hadn't been on my side with love or money. I blamed Pan, and I threw the mask away.

Now somewhere in Brighton Beach, at the bottom of the sea, lies a horned mask with a smile on it with my name carved at the rear, year 1976. I hope Pan has forgiven me for what I did.

I can go on writing another book on signs I've had from the spirit world.

Just to name a few events of the phenomena . . . I've had a tape materialising with new dance songs that the world has not yet heard of. It didn't belong to me and I don't know how it got there. There are sounds of flying saucers in it. I have channelled songs, seen orbs appear in the rear-view mirror of my car, and a woman who astral travels when we think of each other. I have photos shot with a disposable camera to prove the evidence of the orbs and the woman astral travelling, whom I recognise as one of my exes.

My *Phantom of the Opera* album—I found scratches that later disappeared. The same scratches and cracks have appeared on my brand-new CD covers and new reading glasses. I also found a giant mushroom.

I can go on with so many spooky events to justify the puzzle of this mystery that has followed me for centuries.

I have a friend, Jhon, and his wife, Tanya, who call me Master. Others called me the Playboy of Lygon Street, a nickname I didn't know I had until my brother-in-law went to Vietnam and discovered it from some Italians from the Dolce Vita days of Carlton who now live there.

Casanova was passionate, a lover of women and not just a fucker. There are plenty of fuckers around these days, but not lovers like Casanova. He adored the beauty of women and art. He was a free spirit. This is why he could never rest in peace with one woman and live in one place.

This was my story with the evidence to prove it—believe it or not.

This time, I have lived to put an end to the book. Now the spirits of Pan, Casanova, Don Juan, and Valentino have been redeemed. My soul now can finally rest in peace.

Nicholas Arborea

9 April, 2009

I am still mystified about what happened to me since I met Nick. He has been the most honest and straightforward male I've ever met.

It's been a real pleasure and privilege to have known this man. A unique experience that I may never experience in life ever again. Something that I would recommend for any woman to try, if it could be repeated.

A man I will remember forever.

—Rose Squila

PAN

The deity of the pagans, the Arthurians, and the world's most passionate lover of women.

Picture of Pan above unearthed in Pompeii, Italy, near Naples, the ancient city destroyed by the volcano Vesuvius, 79 A.D.

Pan was also seen in Benevento in the area of Naples, dancing with witches around trees. See him on the liquor bottle of "Strega".

In my research in ancient historical and mythological scriptures, I discovered that Pan had previously lived in another life in India, known then as Lord Krishna in 400 BC.

Krishna was also a shepherd who had the same characteristic personality as Pan.

When he blew the flute, virgins fell in love with him, he too like Pan had a countless number of women and married several wives.

I also found a statue of Pan, known as God of Nature 100 BC, amongst the deities and sharleen masters, in Buddhist temple.

Evidence that proves that I wrote about Pan
in my high school magazine.

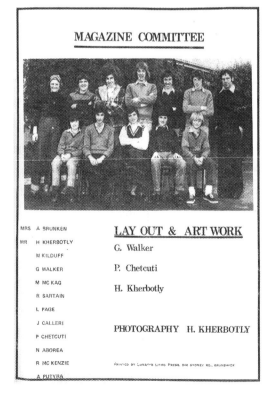

I Dream of A Horned Man

It all started when our art teacher told us to make a paper mache head. Dreaming and thinking about the planets and the living creatures on them, I decided to make a model of what I thought existed far away from our earth. At the end of the week, most students presented good work, there were all different kinds of faces that looked funny, disfigured, strange, mean, and happy. Of all these my work was successful enough to be chosen for the art display at Coburg Town Hall.

Work from every school in the surrounding areas of Coburg district entered. Each student did his best, and I was glad to win the award. The night before that I went to see the art display, my little brother had a bad dream. He explained to me that I was fighting with a man that had HORNS. He told me that I was dying and I slowly disappeared into thin air. Being happy the next morning, because I hadn't disappeared, I went to school. My friend told me that I would never see my paper dream again, he told me that it accidently fell off the car during the transportation of the work from the school. Since then I never saw my dream again.

NICKY ARBOREA 3E

Hume Leader

MORELAND EDITION   TUESDAY, MAY 16, 2006

Tuck into big find

WITH about 40 years of collecting experience under his belt, Nick Arborea of Glenroy thinks his recent find is the biggest mushroom he has ever seen.

"It's like something out of a fairy book," said Mr Arborea.

The giant mushroom was found on a regular autumn trip to the hills around Kangaroo Ground.

Mr Arborea said he had been making the annual trips since he was a boy when he used to go with his father.

The spongy-mushroom was good to eat, according to Mr Arborea but it took special preparation; the removal of the sponge and peeling the skin.

But he warned people to be careful about which mushrooms they picked and where they picked them from. "Try to get them from a safe spot with no metal or broken bottles lying around," said Mr Arborea.

Nick Arborea with his big mushroom. N46HO107

With years of experience the keen collector has learned to distinguish the poisonous varieties from the edible ones.

He said his family would enjoy the mushroom cooked with garlic and chillies.

These are my songs that can be downloaded from iTunes:

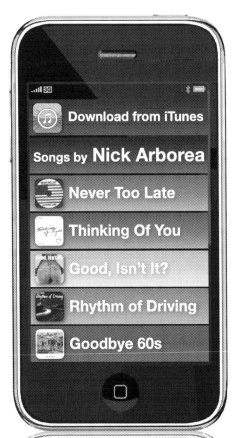

Download from iTunes

Songs by **Nick Arborea**

Never Too Late

Thinking Of You

Good, Isn't It?

Rhythm of Driving

Goodbye 60s

All good songs shouldn't be left unheard.

All of the songs I've channelled during meditation.

CHAPTER 6
The Forbidden Apple

Pan was the first child to be born from Adam and Eve's offspring that the sacred Scriptures didn't tell us about. Those who wrote the first Bible gave us their interpretation of the story about the facts of the truth the way things were at the beginning of time.

I'll tell you my version of the legend of the forbidden apple.

Once upon a time, this world as we know it was pure, without flaws, and everything in life worked in perfect order. Only peace, love, and harmony reigned among nature on earth. The aborigines of Australia called it "Dream Time." Nature's ecosystem would automatically rejuvenate itself effortlessly; it would reproduce anything that was taken from it. The weather was stable: clear-blue skies, sunny, and twenty-five degrees all year around. Adam and Eve didn't have to work for what they needed. God gave them magic to manifest anything that they ever wished for, the creativity to do and keep busy, the secret to heal, and everlasting life.

God did make both of them perfect in his image, taught them ten basic commandments as a simple doctrine to follow, and didn't bash them with anything else.

Eve was warned by God that in the garden of Eden, there would be a serpent that was going to lure her into temptation to have sex with another man, who would appear different but as attractive as Adam. The snake would lead her to the apple tree where she would be introduced to him. She was put on notice not to be embroiled by the false promise to experience greater sexual pleasure.

If she tried that man, she would become insatiable, never to be satisfied by just Adam, and eventually even the Devil would no longer please her. Eve disobeyed God and had sex with the beast. She fell pregnant to him and deceived Adam into believing that the child she was carrying was his.

When Pan was born a freak with the little horns of a goat, Adam and Eve abandoned him in the forest. When Adam asked God why they were being cast on earth, and why their child was half-human and half-animal, God told Adam to ask Eve to provide for an explanation. Eve felt ashamed. She couldn't face Adam at first but then felt compelled to tell him the truth about why Pan was born like that.

At first, Adam was devastated. He didn't talk to her for a few days. He was no longer in love but was hooked by her lust. He eventually forgave her, because he didn't want to be alone. He missed her and feared that she would return to the Devil. But Eve was not happy to be with Adam anymore. Adam asked what he could do to make her happy. She told him that if he wanted to see her happy, he had to allow her to share her love with the other man.

Adam became jealous, but, to keep her happy, he consented to her wish and told her that if she had to have sex with him, he wanted to join in at the same time. And that was when orgies and promiscuous sex began. Since then, all the offspring from Adam and Eve, Cain and Abel, became the sinners of this world, afflicted by adultery, greed, anger, jealousy, laziness, corruption, and evil.

God never abandoned Pan, just like he never abandoned his other lamb, Jesus, when he came down to earth to save our souls, not to exempt us from our sins as we've been misled to believe by those who gave false hope to manipulate the credibility of our faith in God. You'd be foolish to believe that you can do all the wrong things and get away with them. What goes around will come around, and we will all face the music when we return next time. If we are allowed to come back, those who don't believe in God, who believe that they are God, self-made, will not get to see him. But they will see only darkness and remember everything they did with no way to escape their own prison.

Pan was raised and looked after by the little people of the forest; the gnomes, the nymphs, and the fairies became his best friends. When he grew up, they made him their king. God gave Pan the command of nature, love, and passion to please the creative gift of music. The same love and ecstasy that God gave Adam and Eve when he made sex for their pleasure and enjoyment, he left Pan with the secret of the magic to heal and everlasting life. That has been passed on over the ages from Arthur to the alchemist.

Those offspring who came from Pan are those that in society shine among us, those who try to make a difference to resolve the problems of this world. They are those gifted people who are at service to others and care for the benefit of humanity. They are among those who will put their life at risk to put other people's lives first. These are people who have their hearts and intentions in the right place, the seeds to do good works to make the world a better place in the eyes of God.

Pan was wrongly judged by the Catholic Church, demonised, and mistaken for a fallen angel, just like those stunning women who fascinated men with their beauty and then were considered witches who were burned at the stake.

In the book *Angels A to Z,* written by Matthew Bunson, Pan doesn't exist among the list of fallen angels. This information also appears in the rabbinic lore of the Jews.

Many have come from Pan's bloodline, but only a few have been privileged over the ages to inherit his real spirit.

He now lives within some of the crystal children.

Nick Arborea

CHAPTER 7
What I Know about Women

My view on *what women want* cannot be generalised, and I do not expect people to agree. I do, however, speak from facts gathered from personal experiences I've had with women over the years. I know that what you are about to read is easier said than done. But believe me: with a bit of goodwill and practice, a man can make a difference to improve his sex life.

1. **A woman likes to be heard and a man needs to be a good listener.** Particularly at that time of the month when she has PMS, men should keep cool and avoid conflict. She can be very sensitive and aggressive during this period, and she could snap at you when she doesn't mean it. Try to be patient and comprehend her feelings. Do not shout or answer back if she says or does something that gets on your nerves.

2. **Learn about her tastes, likes, and dislikes.** One way of finding this out is by going window-shopping with her. Make comments on what you see in the window and be observant about the things she puts her eyes on to get an idea of what clothes, shoes, jewellery, perfumes, and colours she likes. Never go out there to buy something hoping that she will appreciate it, unless you are a clairvoyant or a good mind reader. Don't waste your money. Most of the time she'll say, "I love it," just to keep you happy. If you are not sure what she wants, buy her a gift voucher—let her choose what she prefers.

3. **Never forget her birthday and St. Valentine's Day.** Always write a nice card and take flowers along, especially on your first date. Always try to be a gentleman by offering to pay the bill. Do not sleaze on, or make a pass on her, on your first date. A good-night kiss on her cheek will do. Unless she is all over you and asks you to sleep over when you drop her off, don't ask for anything. If she wants to see you again, believe me: she will let you know. And she will ask you to return her calls.

4. **In the bedroom, you must make an effort to find the time—no excuse!** Most couples can't be bothered to make time for themselves, to freshen up, and to regain that lost loving feeling between them. It's often the same, lame "too tired" excuse; it's "wham, bam, thank you, ma'am!"

To re-energise the sexual appetite and alleviate distress, you need to make an effort to have a warm, aromatic bath with your favourite oils or soaps. Light up a red or pink candle to generate passionate energy and then cleanse each other like two children playing in the bath. You might end up doing it in the bath, and by the time you get out, all you want to do is go to bed. But at least you've tried something different and you'll sleep better.

Once you get out of the bath, lie next to her and look her straight in the eyes with desire. Start playing with her hair as you gently stroke her body up and down. The tips of your fingers and your hand must caress the body like the touch of a bird's feather to give pleasure and generate healing energy from your fingers.

Then ask her to turn around. Sit nude on her back, with your legs over her butt. Massage her back. Start from the lower back, then move your way up to her neck and shoulders. Apply enough pressure with your fingers. Ask her if she likes it like that or if she wants it harder, gentler, etc. Communication is very important, until you get to know your partner well. As you continue to massage her back, you'll probably get a stiff. If you do not get excited so soon, place the bar between the split of her arse but do not go inside, just make her feel it as you move up and down.

Now it's time to start kissing and nibbling her neck, especially between her neck and shoulders, then lick and kiss the left and right sides of her body, the middle of her back, her spine from top to bottom. Stop with a bite on one side of her leg. Give a gentle bite. Don't leave your teeth marks, which will cause pain.

Now it's time for foreplay. Turn her around. Lick and kiss around her nipples, left and right. From time to time, open your mouth as if you want to eat the whole breast. Try to suck as much as you can. Then continue to kiss her body as you move down toward her vagina. Kiss above it, spread her legs wide open, and put two fingers inside her. Feel her inside—go as deep as you can go to the neck of her vagina, as far as your fingers can reach. By now, she would be wet enough. Then start to sniff the odour of her juice. If you like what you smell, and make sure you have enough light in the room, see if she has any unusual spots like ulcers or warts. If it is safe, then lick the lips of her vagina, left and right. When she starts moaning, lick her G spot fast. When she is ready to make you go inside with your penis, she will certainly let you know about it and say, "Put it inside, now!" Or she will tell you to keep on licking faster or slower, or she'll say she likes it like you're doing.

When you put it in, stay hard, bang her hard at the rhythm she likes, and it is important that you do not come until she does—it's imperative that you try to climax together if you can. Try to come soon after her body is vibrating from her orgasm. Believe me: if you want to please a woman sexually, it's ecstasy and delight if you can come together at the same time. Experts sustain that it's normal to last between three to five minutes. Some say twenty to twenty-five minutes is an acceptable duration for some women. In my view, twenty-five minutes is enough for a woman to start coming. A good lover, in my view, should last between thirty and forty-five minutes.

It takes practice to learn self-control to avoid premature ejaculation. The secret is when your penis goes up, ignore the warmth and vibration she emanates from her vagina. Try not to feel her; just fuck her! Do not connect the mind with your dick, otherwise you are going to come quickly. Is this clear? A cock has a mind of its own. Only you can learn to control it. When you come, roar like an animal. Let it all out! Do not hold inside what comes naturally out of your heart.

Most women don't mind a bit of *dirty words* during the sexercise. Some of them like to know exactly what goes through a man's mind as he is fucking her. If you like to speak dirty, make sure that you warn her beforehand so that she doesn't get offended and knows that it's all in good fun and part of the excitement of your fantasy. A woman enjoys a man who is a little bit creative in the bedroom, who can suggest something different to spice up the relationship.

Most sensual, erotic, feminine females like to dare—try almost anything to the extreme at least once. As long as a man's in control and doesn't go overboard and hurt her. Whatever he suggests can be experimented, only if consented by her and without drugs or being heavily drunk off your face. And never force a woman to do something she doesn't want to do. When she says, "Enough, I can't take it anymore," you withdraw. Stop before someone gets hurt.

An example of a fantasy. A woman with long hair might like her hair gently pulled back, as if she is a horse who is being mounted and pulled back by her cowboy. When she is bending in a submissive position, which most people know as doggy style, she feels safe to play the game, especially when occasionally the cowboy slaps her arse on the side as he is banging her away. When everything is done properly, within limits, she feels in control, and she allows her man to dominate her because she can trust that he is not going to lose self-control.

It would be impossible for any man to discover all the deepest sexual fantasies of a woman. Don't ever believe a woman who tells you that "size doesn't matter." Size *does* matter—and quality too. A man has to have it, and, most importantly, know how to use it. It is imperative that a woman allows her man to probe into her private fantasy world. Women, be totally open. Don't hide anything from him that turns you on. A man likes to know exactly what goes through your mind regarding your sexual desires.

To keep an attractive woman, a man needs to have financial security. "No money, no honey," and that's the cruel reality. Those who have a beautiful woman who doesn't care about money are charmed and have been very lucky in life; it's like winning the lottery. The majority of the women will put money before love and sex—they can get that on the side anytime. Even when a woman has it all, there is no guarantee that a man can keep a good woman tied down. And to keep a relationship going, sometimes one of the two needs to close a blind eye, especially when there are children involved.

And this is all the truth you need to know about women.

Are You a Lover or a Fuck-Her?

Which one are you?

The Lover

He is the real masculine male. Not gay or bisexual. He is a straight, gentle, caring, considerate character who enjoys giving sexual pleasure to women and knows how to satisfy most of them.

He has the natural stamina and endurance to last. He is a very passionate and romantic lover. In the physical form, he comes across as a handsome, rugged-looking type of bloke, not necessarily angelic or stunning.

He has a cheery smile and penetrating eyes that sexually arouse any woman at first sight. His body heat in bed is hot, and his penis is sufficiently well hung.

He is naturally confident and charismatic, not self-absorbed. An individual who often goes out solo, uses his freedom to move around, very sociable, and friendly. Doesn't need his mates at the pub to hold his hand.

He is the smooth operator who knows what to say and do at the right time. He doesn't beat around the bush, as they say. He is not a bullshit artist—a woman always knows where she stands with him.

He doesn't drink or smoke, he is against the use of any drugs, he is health conscious, and he likes to do things naturally on the spur of the moment.

He is responsible and aware of his actions and doesn't like to lose control. He is a good dancer, knows how to dress to impress, and has good taste for real music.

His spirit lives often within the crystal children. He is a pacifist, the tantric and spiritual master, the healer.

He often finds himself arguing and fighting the injustices of this world. He has the right intentions to do good works for the benefit of humanity and cares for the protection of children, animals, and nature.

If rubbed the wrong way and knowing he is on the right side of the natural law of justice, his adversaries will know who they are up against. He stands by the supreme truth.

When he falls in love, he becomes the most reliable, trustworthy male. He will never stray unless he is betrayed by his beloved. When deceived, his wounds will take a long time to heal. He is a sensitive, sensible character, a man with a big heart.

These men have the spirit of Pan in them.

The Fuck-Her

What some women may have dreamed or sexually experienced as a nightmare with some men is the spirit of the fallen angels called Incubus—the seducer fuck-her who brings pain and trauma in women—and the horned spirit called Amadeus—demon of lust, anger, and sexual violence. They were often mistaken for Pan because they disguise themselves as Pan. They too had horns.

Men possessed by one or both spirits aren't all violent but they can be very difficult for a woman to handle and put up with.

These types of men are careless, selfish, inconsiderate lovers, the wham-bang-thank-you-man. Their body heat in bed is cold, and many are very well-hung and whoresome. You'll find this type of character among the control freaks who enjoy inflicting emotional and physical pain in women, and they also go looking for trouble.

This bloke is impatient and has no time for all the pampering and romantic stuff.

These two spirits are greedy, insatiable, materialistic, self-absorbed, dictatorial, vain, and indifferent. They are only concerned about their own sexual self-gratification and financial interest.

You find these characters more among high-profile people, those in positions of power, the rich and famous celebrities fallen from grace. Those are people who have too much of everything.

But all the money and all that they have is never enough—they want more. They can be as attractive as Criss Angel and as hypnotising as the illusionist David Copperfield.

They are empty, shallow men who don't know how to love a woman. Even when they are loved and shown how to love, they can't be bothered. Love for them is just a fuck.

One big, bad habit that they all share in common is to drink until they drop dead, and another is snorting cocaine to get it up. They can't get excited unless their woman is drunk, asleep, or semi-concious, so that she doesn't remember the next day.

A good old Aussie saying is, "Fuck me dead." It comes from people who can't have, or enjoy, sex unless they are dead drunk. This saying is as old as the early settlers.

When the woman would say to their drunken, rough-and-ready partner, "You can fuck me when I'm dead," it meant "when I am dead drunk or asleep."

- In life, there are two types of men: the lover and the fuck-her. Which one are you? I hope you've learned the difference between the two. One has the spirit of Pan. The other has the spirit of a fallen angel or Satan himself.

- There's also an old Italian saying regarding some women who have done it all, been there, and done that: Not even the Devil himself was able to suffice them, but Pan could.

CHAPTER 8
Rubbing Shoulders with the Stars

With Paulo Rossi and teammate, winner of soccer's World Cup
in 1982. I worked as security and tour guide.

Top model Elle Macpherson.
I worked as her security.

Australian actress Fiona Caraffa at
Miss Italy Australia. I was her security.

Lucio Dalla, Italian singer. I worked as security.

With director of the movie *Charlotte's Web*. I was a film extra.

With Zibi Boniak, one of Juventus's greatest players.

The Dalai Lama. I worked as his security.

ELIZABETH TAYLOR

Mr. Nicolas Arborea
157 West St.
Glenroy 3046 Victoria
Melbourne, AUSTRALIA

Nov.18,1987

Dear Nicolas,
            On behalf of Miss Taylor,I want to thank you
for your beautiful flowers. Miss Taylor has appreciated them
very much.
            As far as your story for a film is concerned,
I am sending you the address of Miss Taylor's agent who deals
with these matters. His address is:

                    THE LANTZ OFFICE
                    9255 SUNSET BLVD.
                    Los Angeles,Calif. 90069

            I send you Miss Taylor's best wishes for a suc-
cessful future career.

                              Sincerely Yours,

                              Roger Wall

Gordon L. McKenzie

A.B.N. 31 065 289 210
Teacher Registration Number: 323780
B.Mus. (Melb.), A.Mus.A., C.P.T.R. (Dist), C.M.C.. Cert IV
<u>Authorised Civil Marriage Celebrant A8071</u>
<u>Musician and Entertainer</u>

BOOK SUMMATION

In this no-holds-barred and detailed recollection of a romantic life and a half, of which Casanova and Don Juan would be rightfully boastful, with a tell-it-all philosophy driving the dialogue, Nick leads his readers on a journey through his amazing life of achievements, experiences and romances, with a passion that only those who feel the power of the written word, can fully comprehend.

Gordon McKenzie – Editor, Con Brio.

3 Buckle Road, Toolern Downs, Melton, 3337 Victoria, Australia
Telephone: +61 3 9743-7603 Facsimile: +61 3 9743-7603 Mobile: 0402 144-844
Email: flashgordonmck@corpconnect.com.au
Web- Site: http://abundanceoflight.com/jennyandgordon.html

I've known Nick for many years.

If the walls of my café could talk, I can only imagine what they would say about him!

In his heyday, I've seen him many times around the Little Italy of Carlton, often with different women.

I was envious of The Playboy of Lygon Street, l'artista.

Tony Nicolini

ABOUT THE AUTHOR

Nicholas (Nick) Arborea was born in Italy in 1961. He migrated with his parents to Melbourne, Australia, in 1972. He was educated at Coburg Technical School (Batman College), and graduated with a diploma of architectural and structural design. He also has a diploma of psychology counsellor (The Medical Register of Australia).

Artistically creative since an early age, he has written songs, adult novels, and concepts for new movies. He is an accredited member of APRA (The Australasian Performing Right Association), Author's Association, and Actor's Equity. In the past, he has worked as a tiler, renovator, film extra, and occasionally as a security guard to celebrities. He also worked as a volunteer announcer for radio 3ZZZ and 88.9 WYN FM and a correspondent journalist for an Italian migrant magazine.

After a car accident in 2004 forced him to re-evaluate his life's priorities, he temporarily retreated to Rye on the Mornington Peninsula on the east coast of Victoria. There he writes and paints.

PRAISE FOR NICHOLAS ARBOREA

An amazing true story of an ordinary man with material evidence to prove the facts and the discovery of a mysterious secret behind his extraordinary life. Multi-creative, romantic, sensitive, passionate—how every real man should be.

Shel Angelica, clairvoyant / metaphysician

Many men could learn and benefit from these few tips from you.

Sylvana, pharmacist manager

A man who really knows what women want!

Lisa, executive

The real "Sexiest Man Alive," not some Hollywood character fabricated by some producer or writer of gossip magazines.

Tanya Simone, regular reader of women's magazines

Nick is a tantric master and healer, just what a woman needs.

Daniela Dolce, Nurse

The spirit of Casanova: Nichola Arborea.

Portrait by Charles Billich,
internationally renowned Australian artist